Tap to tidy

to

AT *Pickle Cottage*

To the Pickles, Zachary, Leighton, Rex and
Rose, and to our fur babies, Peanut and
Teddy. And to my extended Instagram
family, thank you for being alongside me
on one of the most magical journeys.

To Theo – we miss you. Pickle Cottage
is not the same without you. Thank you
for the best thirteen years.

STACEY SOLOMON

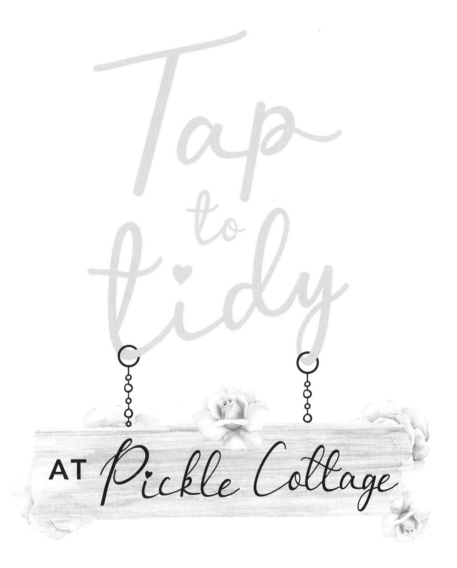

Tap to tidy

AT *Pickle Cottage*

CRAFTING & CREATING
A HOME WITH LOVE

Contents

Making your House a Home

♡

Having your own home is something we all dream about. If you are lucky enough to have your own space, then no DIY or crafting idea is a rubbish one, providing that you love it – 100 per cent. I would never shy away from putting something in my house because it is not 'on trend' or the 'cool thing' to have. I only put in my home what makes me happy, so when I sit there looking at it, or when I use it, it will make me smile. It is never about what other people think. You should be able to walk into your home and do whatever you want with it. It's your home and you deserve nothing less than absolute happiness!

I know how lucky Joe and I are to live in Pickle Cottage with our little family.

Some days I don't believe it is real and this is my life – but my home is wherever my family is. It wouldn't matter to me if we lived in a caravan just as long as we were all together. When Joe bought a campervan, I still put flowers and other nice things inside that made it our home.

With any living space or bedroom, you can always make it 'you'. It doesn't need to be big, posh, or grand. I never felt like my home wasn't my home when we lived in Dagenham, even though I shared a bedroom with my two siblings and my son; I never felt like it wasn't mine. I made the corner of the room that I had my own. I stuck stickers up, made my bed every day

with a special cover, and had my own soft and fluffy blanket; it's those little touches that you put in that make you cosy and content. I genuinely believe that if you put things that make you happy in your space, then it will always feel special and unique. If you are renting a home, you may not be able to make big changes to the fabric of it, but there are loads of things you can do to make your home feel comfortable and yours. Never question yourself. Keep your head and your toes held high!

Special memories, objects from the outdoors, things that remind you of places you adore... that's how I find ideas. I choose colours that I love inspired by plants or flowers that I like, such as lavender and what I call 'swinger's grass' (it's actually pampas grass but when I first started getting it, everyone said, 'That's what swinger's use to let you know their house is open and ready for you!') – I bloomin' love 'em! Sometimes I will go to the beach and have a magical day with the kids and bring back a memento to make something with, or go to a forest and smell an incredible scent and try to recreate that at home. For me, finding associations with moments and memories in your life that make you feel cheerful and bringing them into your living space can recreate those magical vibes every day. Home sweet home. The start of a new chapter.

Don't Be Afraid to Ask

For me, the whole point of doing DIY in my own home is to feel empowered.

There is nothing about having long nails or fluffy slippers that means you can't do it yourself. Believe me. Growing up, it was never an option to hire people to come and do work on our home. Unless my dad physically couldn't do it because it was against the law, like with some electrical jobs, he would do all the jobs around the house himself to save money.

Dad would always ask us kids to help out, show us what to do, and was adamant that we knew how to replace a lightbulb, fix a leaky tap, or change the fuse in a plug. Dad wanted us to know how to do all the basic stuff that might go wrong in a home so we would be able to do it ourselves in the future.

'What are you going to do Stace?' he'd say. 'If you can't afford to call someone out every five minutes, you have to learn to do it yourself.' He was – and still is – the best teacher and we really enjoyed learning to DIY alongside him. We enjoyed the shopping trips less. When we were teenagers, he would drive us to a DIY shop, like B&Q, and pull up outside. As he shut the door, he would always say, 'I'll just be five minutes.' An hour later, my sister, brother and I would be losing the will to live and tearing our own (and each other's) hair out!

Dad wanted us to know how to do all the basic stuff that might go wrong in a home.

Thanks to my dad's DIY lessons, I now do loads of DIY with my boys. They grow in and out of it, but Rex, my youngest boy, loves to help out when I am doing stuff around the house. He knows how to use a hammer and a screwdriver; he doesn't just pretend, he actually uses them properly. Rex has his toy versions of certain tools too, but he is just not that interested in playing. If I try to give him a kid's toy drill, he looks at it and raises his eyebrows as if to say, 'What the hell is that? Who hasn't charged the real drill?!'

Relax, any concerned parents. I always supervise Rex really carefully and obviously would never leave him alone for a single second when he is helping me. I think the quicker you can get your kids into doing DIY for themselves, the more likely it is that they will become independent as they get older. And the sooner you get stuck in, the more confident you will become, too.

I think it's OK not to know everything, as well. I still ring my dad for DIY advice even now. It's OK to admit that there are some jobs you can't do and need to call someone out, such as an electrician or plumber. I don't know how to weld pipes or change taps safely and efficiently – that's what the experts are trained for and what they are there for.

Also, it's OK to call up the staff at DIY stores. When my dad has been away or working and I can't ask him for advice, I ring up places like B&Q, Homebase, or Wickes and ask, 'What would you do for this?' or 'How would you do that?' That's what these stores are there for. I will either ring them up or walk in and ask them to tell me everything they know. They are totally up for it because they do it day-in, day-out and really know their stuff. I don't know if it's a 'me' thing or a British thing, but often I end up apologising loads for asking and they always tell me that they love to help. Never be afraid to ask, however silly you think it makes you sound!

Getting the opinions of others can help when you hit a DIY or crafting hurdle. My family used to joke that 'Dad knows best' because he was always the expert, but us kids are getting so good at DIY now that when we are doing stuff, we'll sometimes make better suggestions. (Sorry, Dad, but it's true!) Even Joe points stuff out sometimes and I wonder why I didn't see it, but he just got there quicker than me. Always ask and chat, because there is always an answer.

In **Tap to Tidy at Pickle Cottage**, I talk through some of the DIY and home improvements that I've made while renovating our new home. I hope this book will inspire you to start your own DIY journey and be a helpful and fun source of practical advice.

CRACK ON WITH IT

Dad gave me so much confidence to do DIY stuff myself. I think confidence comes through taking a deep breath and just doing it. I can't ever remember picking up a drill and feeling totally cool. I had to work it out and do it 100 times before I thought I was really good at it. By that stage, at least I knew that I wasn't going to bring the house down by putting a hole in the wall (yes, I could accidentally drill through a cable or pipe but we'll cover how to avoid that later!). I think having someone to guide you is important, but then putting it into practice is the only way to learn and feel better. If you put ten holes in the wall because you are trying to put a picture up, it's not ideal but you can fill them in and put paint over the ones you don't need and everything will be fine. Just go for it. Then the next time you will only put five holes in the wall!

Making mistakes is so important. We tell our kids all the time that making the odd mistake and then learning from it is a good thing, so why is doing DIY any different? There have been so many times when I have done something and it does not look right at all. The best part of that is I have to figure out what I am going to do instead. The damage control side of my brain then has to get into gear to try and work out what the hell I am going to do next. Once you have made a mistake you aren't likely to make it again and you will find a better way of doing it. Then you feel all creative and good because you are getting on with things yourself, and you won't mind that you made the mistake in the beginning!

CATCH A BREATH

There are so many ways that doing DIY helps me to feel calm and relaxed. When I start a task, first I have to think about how I'm going to approach what I am doing. How do I start? Are there instructions I need to follow? What tools do I need with me to complete the task? Do I need to ask anyone any questions? Then I'll get everything I need and have it all prepared and ready to go. Crafting and DIY makes me feel the way tidying and organising does: it completely focuses my mind and clears my head of everything else when my brain just won't shut up. I think it must be a bit like meditation, although I am not the sort of person who can lie there and take long breaths and do whatever it is you are supposed to do to calm yourself down. That is not me at all.

I love the methodical approach to DIY – by doing each job in different steps, you really can't let your mind wander to other things. If you skip a step the whole thing won't work and you will have to go backwards or start again! Most DIY jobs are really logical and not rocket science once you know what you are doing, and that in itself can be comforting.

If I am worrying and stressing about something, I find that taking myself off to do some DIY works wonders and gives me time to 'catch a breath'. I really do consider it 'me time'. I'll ask Joe to look after the kids for a while, so I can get cracking on whatever job needs to be done. I feel like I am doing something productive, so I'm not 'wasting' time.

It feels so satisfying when you've finished and seen the results of your hard work. A room will start to come together or look great but, not only that, I start to feel better on the inside, too, and more able to carry on with my day, look after the kids, and do my work. It's a win-win-win as far as I'm concerned! All the wins with DIY.

The Story of Pickle Cottage

♡

Joe and I always knew our first home was a starter home as, with four kids between us back then (and five now!), it was relatively small, but it was handy for work because it was so near London. During Covid when we were all stuck at home working, we realised that we didn't need to be quite so close to town and we always said that if a house came up a little bit further out into the countryside, we would keep our eyes and ears open, and think about moving.

We had been looking for ages and ages and missed out on a couple of places. At the time we were really disappointed but sometimes you can't help but feel that some things are meant to be. One day, we were driving along what is now our road, which is basically surrounded by huge fields, and we saw a 'For Sale' sign up outside Pickle Cottage. We couldn't believe it

was for sale; it was the most beautiful grand house and garden. We rang up the estate agents and were expecting them to give us a ridiculous price and when they told us, I almost fainted! It was the same price as our old house.

I couldn't believe we could afford it and that the house even existed! Joe and I did not grow up thinking that we would ever live in a home like that. He grew up in a Housing Association property in Islington and I lived in a two-up, two-down in Dagenham. It just felt like a house like Pickle Cottage would never be on the cards for us. I said to Joe, 'It might mean that we would need to make a bit more of an effort travelling to work but we would have quadruple the amount of space.' We managed to skip a few rungs on the property ladder and I realise how lucky we were to be able to do this,

but by moving a bit further out into the countryside and doing a lot of the work ourselves, we could afford it. The house needed a lot of work and TLC, but I knew I could do it, and the boys are so active and always running around, so we felt we needed to go for it because the outside space is amazing.

I think we got quite lucky because the other people who were interested in it were property developers who wanted to knock it down and build houses on the land. The lady who was living there wanted the house to go to another family to live there and build their lives. She was 93 years old and such a beautiful and kind lady who had raised her entire family there. She was keen to move quickly, so the whole process of moving happened in the space of just a few weeks. I couldn't believe we were going to go for it. Within weeks we had bought Pickle Cottage, sold our house, packed up our belongings and moved. It was a complete whirlwind. We didn't tell many people about it all in case we jinxed it or something!

The first day we got the keys, my dad met us here to help us move in and we all just sat in the kitchen and cried. There wasn't enough Kleenex for all of us! It didn't feel like real life and just seemed far too good to be true. Even now, when I look at the boys running around outside in the garden, I still can't get my head around the fact that it is ours; it's like I have to pinch myself. Once we had been at Pickle Cottage

for a few days, I started dreaming and imagining all the things we could do to make it our home. It started to feel so exciting! Because it's not a listed building and there was nothing in the property of any real historical value, it meant I wouldn't be ruining anything or be taking away from the history of the place if I changed things, so I was completely free to make my own choices. I felt so lucky to have that freedom.

I got started with my renovating and it's been quite a journey so far! There have been some highs, some lows and plenty of cuppas in between. If I'm honest, if you are renovating your house yourself, you are only ever going to feel homey and comfortable in the rooms that you have created when they're done. When you are living in it while you are doing the work, it can feel very claustrophobic and messy. Some days when I looked around and there were no carpets, there was dust everywhere, and it was a complete mess, I wondered what I had started and if I could keep going! I have to be honest about that. I love the fact it's our house, but there were periods when it felt like a complete building site. It's a double-edged sword because, when the place looks like that, it gives me the motivation to do it. It's swings and roundabouts! I know it can feel overwhelming, but I hope my Tap to Tidy DIY methods that work for me will show you how to bring some order to the chaos, too.

MY TOP DIY TIPS

Never wait until tomorrow: With any DIY job, there is always a tendency to put it off. Sometimes it's OK to have days like that, but if you really want to achieve something, you just need to do it. The minute that you start, you will get into it. I promise. Sometimes we all need an initial push to get us on our way!

Be kind to yourself: Doing-it-yourself can be really overwhelming, exhausting and even heart-breaking at times. So, give yourself a break and be kind to yourself when you have those days when it feels like you can't even face anything house-related. That will happen and that is OK. Doesn't mean you have fallen out of love with it, it just means you are working hard!

Don't put pressure on yourself: It's important to be realistic. Most DIY jobs take time. You might want to get it all done yesterday (like me!) but it's better to have clear expectations and know that some things take a little longer, so you won't feel disheartened.

Throw yourself into it: Get stuck into researching and finding out everything you can about what you want to achieve. There is nothing better than having some solid knowledge behind you and appreciate what it is going to take to achieve your dream home.

Set some goals: Try to have some kind of vision of what you want the end result to look like so that you can set yourself some small targets or goals.

Grab your toolbox: Make sure that you have everything you need before starting any DIY job. Before you even begin any project, kit yourself out with the essential tools and then every time you want to do a little DIY, you only have to grab your toolbox and everything you need will already be in there. I have added some handy equipment checklists throughout this book to help you get to grips with what tools you might need for certain DIY jobs.

How to

USE THIS BOOK

This book is for you, the reader, to use as a practical guide, as creative inspiration, or even just to read for pleasure without any pressure to do anything at all! Grab a cuppa and dip in and out of the chapters at your leisure. Most of all, I want you to know that you really do have the skills and the confidence to do anything you want – don't let anyone tell you otherwise. And if you want a glittery table or a seashell picture frame in your home, you should just do it.

I love learning how to do all this stuff – like being able to sand wooden floors, hang picture frames, or put up floating shelves! It's empowering just to get stuff done and to know that even if I make mistakes – and trust me when I say, I make loads – that I can depend on myself. I am not waiting for ages for expert tradespeople to come and quote for the smallest jobs. Yes, I do use them when I need to because there are always certain jobs that I can't do myself (couldn't see me and my pregnant belly digging out the swimming pool!) but there are loads of things I can do safely and quickly. When I do DIY stuff, I just crack on with it – and you can too. Best of all? It saves loads and loads of money. Even if you don't like something you've done, you can just do it again, knowing that you haven't spent a fortune on it.

In a moment I will show you my Tap to Tidy DIY Method and, in each section, I outline how I tackled different rooms in Pickle Cottage. Look out for:

Hero Projects: These are the bigger renovation or organisational projects that might take slightly longer and a few more specialist tools.

Quick Fixes: Do you have a couple of hours to spare? Kids at school or baby having a nap? These are focused and small jobs to spruce up a room.

Make-Ups: Make-ups are my transformative craft projects and accessories to make any room your own and somewhere you love. The only limit is your imagination! Dream big!

Little Things I Love: Power tools, amazing DIY products, my favourite accessories... I tell you all about the stuff that makes me happy and what makes me so excited (it's actually not normal!).

Tips: I'm not a complete expert when it comes to DIY, and let me tell you, I've made some mistakes in my time. So these are my tips – learnt the hard way – to make your projects run smoothly.

How-To's: These are my simple and practical guides to DIY hacks. Using a drill, ripping up carpet, choosing paint colours... and everything in between.

Expert Help: There are always times when you need to call in the experts. I highlight where I have hired tradespeople to do those jobs I can't.

Hopefully, **Tap to Tidy at Pickle Cottage** will give you the confidence to tackle DIY jobs around your own home, but also how to gain inspiration and make your ideas become reality.

The Tap-To-Tidy DIY Method

Step 1: START SMALL

I began with the downstairs toilet first because it was the smallest space and the least daunting. Big spaces can sometimes feel a bit dead and cold. I knew I could complete this room myself and could get started straight away without needing any expert help. I would be able to do it in a short space of time, so the pay-off would be almost immediate, and I wouldn't need to spend lots of money because I didn't need to make any major changes.

For me, I felt that if I started anywhere too big, where the plumbing, electrics, and heating cause problems, it would be disheartening and I knew it would bring me down and make me feel like I couldn't do it. The downstairs loo's small space had none of those challenges – all it needed was a lick of paint, a bit of carpet pulled up, and I would be ready to go. And I couldn't wait to spend some alone time in there once it was finished! Sometimes when someone yells my name, I just sit there with my cuppa and say: 'I'm on the toilet, obviously: not now!'

Step 2: GET THE KIDS COMFORTABLE

For any parent or carer, having your kids comfortable and happy in their own home is the most important thing. The boys wanted to share a bedroom at first, but Dad reminded me that when my sister Jemma and I were growing up, we shared a room and absolutely hated each other. We argued. All. The. Time. About everything. One day we came home from school and Dad had put a wall up. It was smack bang in the middle of the window but Dad was like, 'Right, I have had enough. You can have your own rooms now!' It was much better after that!

The room that my two oldest boys, Zachary and Leighton, wanted to share was massive, so Dad put up a stud wall in the middle with a connecting door so they can still visit each other really easily. Leighton also has a bunk bed, so he can always have his friends to stay over.

We also decided to have some fitted furniture, including wardrobes and desks, put into the boys' rooms. They were expensive but I know that quality furniture will last them a long time and these will be their forever wardrobes. They took a while to be delivered but they fitted perfectly because they were completely made to order.

I have so many wonderful childhood memories of my home growing up. I also have great memories of my mum changing things around at home. They were never massive things but we would come home from school and she would have added a picture, put up a shelf, or moved the furniture around in our bedrooms. I would be so excited about it. I really want my kids to make the same sort of amazing memories here at Pickle Cottage.

Step 3: DO A ROOM YOU LOVE *(one you'd love to live in!)*

The next room I tackled in Pickle Cottage was the conservatory. The light in this room makes me so happy. We moved in the spring and I knew that I wanted it ready for the summer, so I could sit and enjoy the amazing views of the garden. It's also a general living space: the kids play there and I can sit and relax there, too. I'm always bringing in Rex's high chair, so he can eat his breakfast looking out at the flowers and trees.

Like the Blue Loo and Rex's bedroom, I knew I wouldn't need to do loads of building work, so it would be quite straightforward. I did it all myself, apart from some fitted furniture that a carpenter made for us for storage and seating.

I also wanted to create a space where we could all go when the rest of the house was dusty with bigger and messier projects. I knew it would give me somewhere to escape to, so I could enjoy my cuppa in peace. There is a lot of glass in here and I bought Joe a special window cleaning tool – I pretended it was for me but actually it was for him! He loves it! When the glass is completely clear, I just love being in this room. Sometimes I sit in the conservatory at night and can see the stars. It feels so peaceful.

Step 4: MAKE DO AND MEND

Sometimes when you come to look at a room, it can feel hard to know what to do first. For me, I always think about one wall at a time and think about how I can use what is already there and make do and mend. So, for Rex's room this was the fireplace, in Rose's nursery it was the panelled wall, and in the family bathroom it was a wall with the sink unit in it.

When it came to doing the bathroom, there was an old piece of furniture in there. We were in the process of buying new wardrobes for the boys' rooms, so I knew how much quality units cost and I wasn't just going to get rid of the 50-year-old sink cabinet. So that's the wall I did first and after that I found that the rest of the room just flowed. We painted the dark wood black and decided to go with a black-and-white theme. I think monochrome is perfect for bathrooms because it is so fresh.

So my advice would be: if you don't know where to start on a room and feel a bit overwhelmed or not quite sure where you are going with it, just look at one wall and think, 'Is there something I can do with whatever is there?' 'How am I going to do that?' or 'How can I make the wall work?' When I take this approach I tend to find that the rest of the room just follows.

Step 5: THINK ABOUT OUTSIDE

Our garden at Pickle Cottage is the garden of dreams and we were so lucky that it was in such good shape when we moved in; as a result, we haven't had to do much. Also, I am no gardener – let me tell you. But, having said that, if you are renovating the inside of your home, it makes total sense to think about the outside. If your inside is messy and dusty, there is nothing more satisfying than grabbing the jet wash and cleaning an area outside. It will be done in about five minutes flat with minimal effort, and if you can spruce something up it feels so good. I just love jet washing!

I also think it's just as important to work on any structures that you have outside. When I first clapped my eyes on the cute Wendy house in the garden, I almost couldn't believe it. What I would have done for one of those when I was growing up! It made complete sense to revamp this playhouse but I would say the same for any shed, or outside building. Loads of people are working from home now, so if you have the space outside, use it. I plan to turn another shed in the garden into a crafting shed and my office, so I can get away from it all. It will be just me and my glue gun!

Step 6: GET EXCITED (and keep going!)

If you are lucky enough to have the space, create a room just for you! I know sometimes that DIY can feel tiring and a bit relentless, especially if you are doing lots of different rooms at the same time, but if there is any way you can get excited and give yourself some extra motivation, then do it!

Creating my little girl Rose's nursery just felt so special. There were times when I felt overwhelmed by the pregnancy and the demands of work. Being able to go into this room and craft or do some DIY really took my mind away and helped me relax. I love the colour pink and miss my old pink utility room at our previous house so, so much; this room gave me an opportunity to inject some serious pink back into my life and, to be honest, this was just for me.

You could do this with any room or even a corner of a room in your home; it doesn't necessarily need to be a nursery. If you have a spare room, box room, or even a garage space that needs jazzing up, get excited about it. Get creative and do whatever it is that makes you feel good. Don't ask. Don't apologise. Just get cracking!

Step 7: FIND JOY IN THE PRACTICAL SPACES

This step is all about renovating those rooms in the home that make our lives easier. For me, it was the utility room at Pickle Cottage. The amount of washing in my house is an absolute nightmare. There are five kids, Joe, and the dogs and so to keep on top of the laundry is just a horrendous state of affairs. School uniform, sports kits, home clothes, pyjamas, babygrows, oh my goodness... it never ends! I love where we live, with the beautiful fields that surround the cottage, but there is so much mud all the time. So this was all about creating a practical utility room that works for me.

I know I am so lucky to have my utility room and when I was building it, I wanted it as big as possible. I said to Joe that I would rather sacrifice hall space and have a tiny hallway if I could have a massive utility room for the washing. I've also tried to make the hallway a really functional and bright space so our routines, and comings and goings are stress-free.

Step 8: CREATE SOME CALM

I think it is really important to create your own slice of heaven in your bedroom. The bedroom is so important. I knew I wanted it to be a kid-free space, and just ours. The rest of the house is theirs whether we like it or not! We love it but there has to be somewhere in the house that is only for us. It was important to have somewhere bright and light, where we can relax at the end of every day and go, 'We've done it and we're all still alive!'

I think you should do exactly what you want with the space. For me, this was having a free-standing bath under one of the windows. Here, I can have 'thrush baths' and look out at the view. (This is what I call baths that are so hot and full of colourful salts that I reckon they will probably give me thrush, but it's always worth it.) Bliss!

Step 9: SAVE THE BIG STUFF UNTIL LAST

The biggest renovation jobs usually cost the most money so often need to be budgeted and saved for over a period of time. For us, the big stuff was building a small extension on the corner of the house and installing a new kitchen. The kitchen at Pickle Cottage was old and just didn't work for our family and the process of designing a new one was so exciting.

For any building or renovation work, you also have to book your builders well in advance because so many companies are very busy. What's more, if you need to apply for planning permission, this can also take time to be approved. Most kitchen furniture and equipment will also have long lead times, so you will also need to order everything well in advance of it being fitted.

Of course, if you are planning a big house renovation, installing a kitchen will probably need to be done before the other rooms but, in our case, leaving it until last worked out really well. I was able to crack on with the rest of the house, whilst waiting for this bit to happen later.

When it came to doing our work, the timings got pushed back a bit. I had hoped to have it done for the time baby Rose arrived, but it wasn't to be. I think this often happens, so you just have to roll with it. I did love designing and planning this space in Pickle Cottage. I feel it really is true when they say your kitchen is the most important room in your house. It can be the beating heart of it, where you sit and share mealtimes with your family every day, so I wanted to take the time to make it perfect.

The Blue Loo

I love the downstairs
Blue Loo – I'm so
proud of it. I feel all
fancy in there.
I put a little bow in
the loo roll and fold
my towels. It's the
show toilet!

If you have one, everyone sees your downstairs loo. It's not a nothing room; it's one of the most important rooms in the house because everyone who comes to your house is going to need a wee at some point.

There is a slim-to-none chance of guests going to use the upstairs bathroom unless you send them up there yourself! People may enjoy spending time and socialising in a kitchen but the loo is where I spend my quality time! If I want to get away from the kids and Joe, it's where I go for as long as I can get away with, before someone calls my name.

The first thing I did in the Blue Loo was to take everything out of the room and rip up the old red carpet left by the previous owner. With four boys who miss the toilet almost every time they use it, I knew I needed something on the floor that was a bit more durable and that could be wiped down. Once the carpet was up, I could see what I was working with.

The room has this beautiful blue-patterned enamel sink and toilet, which I love. It is so posh! It has a pull chain and everything! It was too special to not build the rest of the room decoration around it. I decided to do all the work around the decorative toilet and sink to enhance the blue pattern and that's how I chose the colour and theme for this room.

I always think working with what you've already got is the easiest way to begin – if you think you have to buy everything new and change everything, not only do you spend a lot more money but it's much more overwhelming to get started. The sink and toilet needed a bit of a clean and revamp, but I could see that they were treasures worth keeping and just needed some TLC. It meant I didn't have to think too hard about what I wanted in there. The theme and the colour were quite obvious to me from the start.

Where
to Start

When it comes to the important stuff, heating,
electrics, and plumbing are the big ones.
You need to consider all these main things
before doing anything else.

If you must rewire, your electrician will need to get behind your walls, so
there is no point in doing anything else until this is done. Likewise, anything
that involves a water supply and waste pipes will interfere with the whole
fabric of your room, so everything needs to be in place and safe before you
start painting or doing other things. Other than these big areas – heating,
electrics, and plumbing – I really do believe that you can learn to do anything
else yourself.

In my own bedroom, I knew I wanted a rolltop bath in there. For that, we would
need a whole lot of new pipework installed, so I couldn't do anything before
it was done. There was literally no point doing anything else beforehand, as it
would all be ripped up again.

The downstairs loo room did not need
anything major doing, so I knew I could
get started straight away.

CHOOSE PAINT COLOURS

As I mentioned, I knew immediately that I wanted to use a blue paint in this room because of the posh enamel sink and toilet. Sometimes if I don't know what I want, I'll create a mood board to help me feel inspired, but here the colour theme came to me straight away.

If there is not an obvious colour to choose for a room, think about the colours you associate with the things you love. It can be anything: green for the garden; blue for the sea or sky; a pastel shade for a baby blanket your kid had; family heirlooms; a colour you love in a friend's house... anything really. I talk a bit more about creating a mood board later on (see page 236).

The blue decoration inside the enamel sink is very dark, almost navy, and I did consider whether to have more of a navy on the walls but I thought it was too dark for the small space. If it had been a bigger room, I probably would have gone for it. In the end, I went for a blue shade for the walls that was the same tone as the decorative pattern but lighter, and white paint for the ceiling.

There wasn't that much choice in the DIY store; I don't go to the posh paint places that often. I do if they have an unusual colour that I really want, but if I know I just want a straightforward blue, I go into B&Q, Homebase, Wickes, or wherever, and choose one of their off-the-shelf blues that is the closest match. You could be deciding on paint shades for bloomin' ages and, personally, I don't think it is worth the energy! I used 'tough and washable' from Wickes on the walls and standard white ceiling paint.

Resist the temptation to come home with a hundred tiny paint pots to start doing those random swatch tests, as they never look the same as when the whole room is painted properly – I sometimes end up even more confused and indecisive when I use tester pots. On the occasions that I do get them, I have to rely on my Instagram family to help me make a decision. I'd be standing there all day trying to decide!

One bit of advice I would give is that if you do use tester pots, instead of painting on the walls, simply paint swatches onto A3 paper that you can move around the room to see how the light changes the colour depending on where it falls. There are some newer mail-order paint brands that will supply you with stick-on panels or peel-and-stick swatches in their paint shades; you can move these around and attach them to different walls to see how the colour looks in different lights.

In the downstairs loo, I painted the ceiling first (as there are always some drips) and then whacked on a couple of coats of blue on the top two-thirds of the walls. I then cladded the lower sections of the walls with tongue-and-groove boards. I talk more about how I tackle painting walls as we go on but, if you want to skip ahead, basically I grab a small foam roller and I simply start painting.

Cladding walls – even wonky old ones!

Hero task

While I was thinking about paint colours for the downstairs loo, I started looking at photos of bathrooms on Pinterest and saw people were painting walls two colours – dark on top and light on the bottom – which has the effect of making a room look larger and brighter.

The loo is already a small room and I didn't want the strong blue colour to make it feel even smaller still, which I worried it would if I painted the same shade over all of the walls. I also spotted that people were dividing up the colour neatly using dado rails. These are rails that are fixed horizontally to the wall at around waist height (if the rail is higher up – around 30 to 50cm (12 to 20 inches) from the ceiling – it is called a picture rail). I wasn't planning to use dado rails at first because some panelling (which I now know is called cladding) caught my eye, but they came in handy with my wonky walls to finish the look off.

I decided to clad the lower half of the walls with white panels to add an extra texture as well as to contrast the blue paint I planned to put on the walls. I felt it would give the room a special touch, making it look like I had spent more time and money on it than I really did!

It is just so easy to put up cladding! SO EASY. It is important to check for damp first as putting cladding over damp walls can make them worse but, despite being an old house, there were no damp issues at Pickle Cottage, so I just went for it. I didn't even have to cut any wood. Instead, I used pre-cut MDF panels, which you can order in different lengths so you don't have to cut it or try to make it level.

Don't overthink it, lovelies!

- **Clear the room of any clutter**, including from the floor. Any toys or other things you might break your neck on – get them out!

- **Make sure your walls are clean**. If they are a bit grubby, wipe them down. My walls were pretty clean but if yours aren't, use sugar soap, which comes in liquid or powder form. It is like a mild detergent and is great for getting rid of any grime that may affect the finish. Sugar soap is better than normal cleaning products like washing-up liquid because it doesn't leave behind a grimy residue. Simply dilute it in warm water and wipe the areas with a cloth or sponge and then rinse with clean water. Allow plenty of time for it to dry before doing anything else. Easy!

- **Work out how much cladding you need** by measuring the width of each wall and adding those measurements together to give you the perimeter of the room. Next, divide that perimeter measurement by the width of the individual cladding panels to give you the number needed. Or you could just take the measurements into the DIY store and they will tell you what you need. The cladding I chose came in packs of ten, so I bought enough packs to give me the number of panels that I needed, plus an extra pack. My top advice is always to buy an extra pack or two because as long as the pack isn't open, you can take it back to the store for a refund. There is nothing worse than getting to the end and realising you are one panel short! Nightmare!

- **Choose your preferred cladding**. You can choose from a range of sizes and colours. I used pre-primed MDF tongue-and-groove cladding, which just needed to be painted. There is also the option of uPVC cladding, which is wipe-clean and doesn't need treating. This type of cladding panels, which interconnect, are called tongue-and-groove boards because each board has a tongue along one long edge and a corresponding groove on the other edge, so the tongue slots into the groove of the next piece.

- **Plan the positions of the cladding panels**. On the back wall, behind the loo, I started the cladding in the middle of the wall and worked outwards into the corners. On the side walls, I started from the corner nearest the door and worked towards the back wall. In the corners, where the space left was too narrow for a full panel, I cut each panel down to fit the space.

- **Fix the first cladding panel to the wall**. On the side wall nearest the door, I placed the grooved edge of the cladding panel flat to the corner of the wall to keep it as straight as possible. Everything will look 'off' if the cladding is not completely straight, so use a spirit level to make

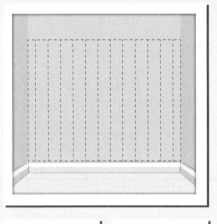

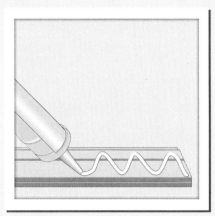

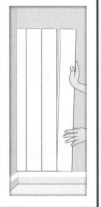

MEASURE UP FIRST (AND GET THE DIY STORE TO CUT ANY PANELS YOU NEED)

If you have the measurements, hardware shops like B&Q and Wickes will cut the panels for you, to any length. Such a great service! They cut any type of wood – cladding, skirting, dado rails – and it's free! Bonus! Few walls are uniform and straight, so you might have to cut down the panels, but DIY stores can do a lot of that leg work.

sure the panels are vertical. To fix the panels in place, I used heavy-duty mounting adhesive from No More Nails – I ran it down the back of the panels before slotting each one into place. Basically, run a zigzag line down each panel before sticking it firmly to the wall.

- **Adjust each panel as you go** to make sure they lie flat against the wall. If you are doing up an old house – or any house that is not completely new and plastered and skimmed – the walls will be uneven, so you have to adjust each panel individually. I do this by just looking at them and standing back to see if they look right. It is never going to be perfectly flat against a wonky surface. Even when walls are newly plastered, you can't ever guarantee they'll be perfectly straight. For me, there were some tricky bits near the loo where the wall had bowed so it was uneven. For uneven walls, it is sometimes recommended that you construct a framework from battens to mount the cladding onto but my feeling is that it would take a lot of skill to do this to make it completely flat. Even if it was a few millimetres out you would have to construct the battens accordingly and it would take a skilled carpenter to do this. I got a long bit of wood and wedged it between the cladding panels that were threatening to pop up, to keep them in place while the glue dried. I kept the wood up for a day to make sure it was all fixed in place. If you

are worried about panelling pinging up unevenly, wedge it in! And don't be tempted to see if it has stuck for at least 24 hours. It's a bit like baking a cake; it's annoying having to wait but you have to be patient!

- **Cut down any panels to fit**. I needed to cut two panels to fit into the corners of the back wall, but I also needed to cut the panels down around the sink. I find straight cuts much simpler to do. Going around pipes wasn't easy so I asked my dad for some help. We used a marker pen to draw on the panels where the cuts needed to be made and then used a jigsaw to cut out the shapes. You do need to be precise as the panel will be on show. (I was glad I had some spare panels as I messed it up the first time.)

- **Finish the cladding with caulk**. When the panels are in position and the glue has dried, apply a thin line of caulk along the top and bottom edges to tidy it all up. I talk about caulk more (see page 114), as I love how it hides no end of imperfections.

- **Paint the cladding**. My panels were already primed, but I knew they would get a lot of dirty marks so I wanted to cover them in plain white paint that could be wiped down. I use a satin emulsion that is a bit glossy when painting wood so it is easier to clean. Satin and gloss paint (see page 59) hides any imperfections better, as well as being more durable.

Little things I love ♡

SAWS

I love well-designed hand tools – they are genius! If you are using them a lot, a good hacksaw and jigsaw are a great investment. Rather than buying it straight away, I hire a saw first to see how I get on with it so I am not taking on unnecessary costs. The general rule is: if you will use something more than three times, then it is worth shelling out to buy it. These must-have tools are not scary; just put some protective goggles and gloves on, stay calm and take your time. I use a hacksaw a lot and I've not cut my arm off yet! As long as you are sensible, there is no reason why you can't get cracking.

HACKSAW: I use a hacksaw all the time, which is a type of hand saw. They are cheap to buy and easy to use. A hacksaw can cut through really tough materials, like metal. Just make sure you use the right blade for the material you are cutting.

JIGSAW: Designed specifically to make non-straight or curved cuts, a jigsaw can cut through all materials. It has a flat base to lean on, so feels safe and is great even for beginner DIY-ers. Make sure you understand how everything works before using.

CHOP SAW: My dad keeps his heavy-duty chop saw at my house. This is the big gun of saws, designed to cut through tough materials like wood, metal, and brick. It is not a tool for beginners.

KEEP GOOGLING!

When searching for DIY products online, try to use the right keywords for the best selection. I didn't know that cladding was called cladding when I first started looking. I was searching for 'planks that go on walls', 'wooden wall fixings', 'panelling'. I even searched for 'bits of wood that lock together with ridges'. So, don't be afraid to put in whatever you're thinking in your head because you will eventually come across the right words to describe what you're looking for. Nothing is too silly!

Cladding, dado rails, lino, herringbone... these are all words that I have learnt during the process of renovating Pickle Cottage. It's like a whole new language! Once I knew exactly what I needed, I looked for 'white interlocking cladding', or 'thick cladding' or 'thin cladding' to try to find exactly the style I was after.

I get an idea of what I'm after and then either buy it in the shops or online. I don't think there's much difference between the two. The reason I went out and bought the cladding from the DIY store is because I wanted it immediately rather than wait for three working days for it to arrive. That said, for hardware products like cladding, most of the time I find DIY stores are cheaper than online retailers because they buy the stuff in such huge volumes. DIY stores also make it easy for you to shop there – you can check online to find out what your local branch has in-store before you go if you want to, and you can do a click and collect if you're in a rush. There are loads of ways to make it all much easier.

There are even cheaper ways of getting wood products, like cladding, such as going to a wood merchant to cut the wood into panels or even cutting the panels yourself. For me, I knew I wanted interconnecting panels to make the job straightforward.

Quick fix

DADO RAILS

Dado rails can look really fab. I wanted one in the Blue Loo because I think it makes the room look bigger. I knew I had to break the walls of the room up a bit and the dado rails and cladding definitely do that. The ledge of the dado rail draws the eye upwards. As we live in a cottage, the ceilings are low in places and there are loads of wooden beams, but because of the dado rails, it doesn't feel like that in the Blue Loo.

Originally, I didn't think I would put a dado rail in this room, but with the walls not being even, the cladding was never going to be perfectly straight along the top edge when I had finished. The dado rails cover up all the gaps and neaten everything up.

❦ Before you put up the dado rail, measure the walls of the room. If you're just doing a rail (without cladding) and are unsure of the height that it needs to be placed, the general thought is that it should sit about a third of the height of the room from the floor (with two thirds above) – but again, do what suits you!

❦ Cut your dado rail to the right length using a hacksaw or chop saw (see page 36). You will need to cut your dado at a 45-degree angle at the end, so the pieces meet at the corners. You can do this by marking the cut using a protractor, but some saws have angles built into them to make it easier. If you get it slightly off, you can fill any gaps with sealant, so don't worry.

❦ The dado rail I used had a lip or a slight ridge, so I popped it over the top of the cladding and fixed it in place with heavy-duty mounting adhesive. If you just have a dado, position it carefully and mark it with a pencil before sticking it down. I would use a spirit level to make sure it is straight, if I didn't have the cladding as a guide. Stick the edges where they meet at the corners, scraping away any excess glue as you go.

❦ Once the dado is on and dry, it's time to get out the caulk to fill in any of the gaps between the dado rail and the cladding. Most sealants use the same kind of applicator as the adhesive. Apply the sealant in a thin line along the top and bottom edges. Job done!

Little things I love ♡

HEAVY-DUTY MOUNTING ADHESIVE

This is a glue, but is a strong adhesive that can hold most things up on the wall providing they are not really, really heavy. The glue I use is called No More Nails, but there are plenty of other brands out there. It is essential for any DIY project, if you ask me!

Once you have put the adhesive into the cartridge gun applicator, it's a doddle to apply. It is different from superglue (and nails), which, when they are in or on, are fixed immediately. With heavy-duty mounting adhesive, if you feel like you are going slightly out of line or a bit wonky, there is some movement because it won't harden in place for about 24 hours. I find that so helpful because nothing is ever perfect when I am doing it, so I can give things a nudge here or there as I go along, until I think it's as good as I can get it.

Quick fix

SPACE-SAVING SHELVES

When I had finished painting the walls and cladding, I did feel like the room needed something 'extra'. It was a bit cool and icy! I had some pampas grass in a Primark vase, and I tried to find some floating wooden corner shelves on Amazon with the same tones in them. I felt it brought a bit of warmth into the room. Floating shelves are such clever little inventions and so much easier to fix to the wall than people think.

❦ All these shelves come with brackets with two or more poles sticking out that will slot in to pre-drilled holes in the shelf to support it. Put your bracket up against the wall where you want it. I put the base on top of the dado rail, so I knew it would be straight.

❦ Before you start thinking about drilling holes for the screws, check for any pipes or electrics behind the walls. There are special electronic testers that do this which are cheap and easy to use. There should be one of these in every good tool kit. No one wants to go through a pipe to put up some shelves! Run it over the area, so you know you are safe to get started.

❦ Place your bracket against the wall and draw a pencil mark into the holes where the screws need to go. You might want to use a spirit level to ensure that the lines are completely level.

❦ Choose the correct size rawl plug and drill bit for your screw. The rawl plugs and screw should be a nice fit – too tight and the rawl plug will snap, too big and it will fall out. Often screws will come with the correct rawl plugs. Make sure they are the right screws for the material of your wall.

❦ Hold the screw up to the drill bit, so you know how far you need to go in. Put a bit of tape to mark the drill bit, so you know not to go further than the mark.

❦ Drill the holes with the drill level and square to the wall and keep your hand as steady as possible, so you drill at 90 degrees and the hole is straight and horizontal.

❦ Put the rawl plug in. It should be a cosy fit, and you might have to tap it with a hammer it so that it is flush with the wall surface.

❦ Screw your bracket on loosely, using a screwdriver, but only half-way in so you can check that the nails are all correct and in line. Once you are happy, screw the bracket flat to the wall. You might want to do this with the drill – just make sure you put the right head on the drill.

❦ Slide your shelf onto the bracket. Put your accessories on the shelves.

❦ Remember to not overload floating shelves – they are pretty sturdy, but I wouldn't place anything too heavy on them.

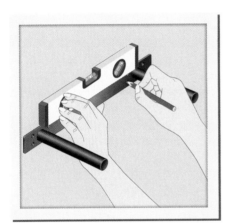

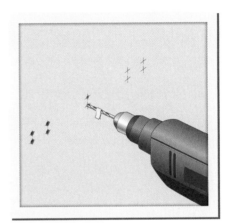

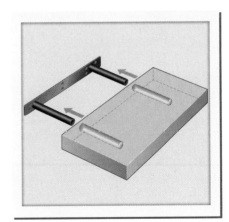

HAVE A GOOD SCREW

Most shelving kits will come with their own screws and rawl plugs, but I prefer to use my own really good quality ones as they tend to last longer. I find the ones that come with DIY packs a bit crap. I genuinely feel that for the sake of spending an extra 10p or 50p, it is worth it to put your own screws in. A good screw is one that you have bought from a DIY store or hardware shop, like Screwfix.

When I was in my early 20s, my dad bought me a toolbox that keeps loads of my DIY stuff together. It's a plastic one with tonnes of compartments and pull-out trays. A bit like one of those amazing make-up boxes but for screws instead. You may also want to buy a mixed pack of wall fixings, which will have loads of good quality screws, nails, and rawl plugs. Like a Pick 'n' Mix of fixings, basically.

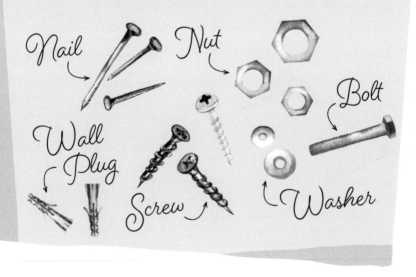

Nail   *Nut*   *Bolt*

Wall Plug   *Screw*   *Washer*

How to

CHOOSE THE RIGHT DRILL BIT

Make sure you choose the right drill bit – this is the piece that goes into the drill to make the hole in the wall. My drill is only a cheap one I bought from IKEA but has all the different drill bits for specific materials. So, a brick drill bit goes into bricks and a tile drill bit drills tiles. There are bits for wood, metal, and one called a masonry bit that goes into concrete, stone, bricks, and plaster. Those are the big guns of drill bits. Also, make sure you use the right size drill bit – measure the screw up against the size of the hole first. The size of the hole should be slightly smaller than the size of the screw.

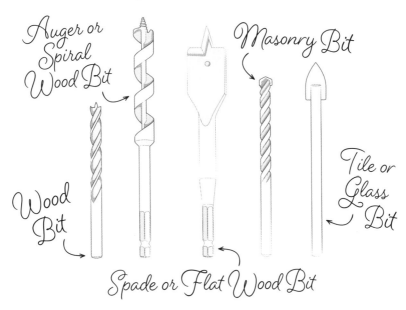

Auger or Spiral Wood Bit

Masonry Bit

Wood Bit

Tile or Glass Bit

Spade or Flat Wood Bit

How to

ORGANISE YOUR BATHROOM BITS 'N' BOBS

In my bathroom, I always have some toilet cleaner and a cloth or sponge just for cleaning that area (so you don't end up getting confused and using it to clean the dishes with!). I put everything into a neat caddy with an air freshener and spare toilet rolls, if there is space. I like to keep my bathroom cabinets simple. If space is limited, I will put the loo rolls in a little basket, which I keep well stocked, and next to the loo for easy access, so you are never left mid-hover trying to grab it! I always put a diffuser on the window sill, to keep the air fresh. Being in a house of boys means that this is non-negotiable!

Quick fix

POLISHING AND CLEANING METALWORK

I love my little sink. It is just so cute and pretty! When I first got to the sink and loo, the brass metalwork around the taps and pipes was green because of the water and air damage over time. Brass is such a resilient metal to have in the house. It may look disgusting if it's not cleaned, and you might think it needs getting rid of, but with a bit of work it comes up a treat – super shiny and just like new.

The most effective cleaning method for metal depends on what type you are working with. With chrome, for example, you can just wipe it with a cloth and normal kitchen cleaner and it comes up shining, but brass needs more elbow grease to make it perk up. I've heard you can clean it with ketchup, but I stuck to the shop-bought brass cleaner! This is what I did:

♥ Get a really fine metal-cleaning soft cloth and some brass polish.

♥ Simply rub a thin coat of polish onto the brass and work it in, using the cloth, to all the nooks and crannies. I started from the top and went down with each fixture I tackled.

♥ Once you've worked the cream all the way down the pipes, wipe back up using the same cloth to reveal the super shiny clean brass underneath!

♥ Sit on the loo, have a cup of tea and admire your handiwork. So satisfying.

Tip

DON'T BE AFRAID TO RE-DO STUFF

Once you've completed a room, you may have to go over certain bits. It can take a while for the dust to settle and stuff can move around a little. Whether you need to go over a spot with a bit of paint, re-seal an area, or have another go at something, it is nothing to be worried about. It's totally normal and OK. That's the fun of DIY. You've not spent your life savings on it, so don't stress out.

Expert Help ♡

FLOORING

I had a flooring company come and put
in the herringbone pattern lino floor.
I got the cheapest flooring I could possibly
find because, with a house full of boys, it
would not be money well-spent if I bought
something better. It cost me around £80 plus
the fitter's time to glue it in place. It's super-
easy to clean with no ridges where dirt can
collect and it matches my shelves. I love it!

MY TOOLBOX
Checklist

- ☐ Hammer
- ☐ Screwdrivers
- ☐ Tape measure
- ☐ Electric drill
- ☐ Spirit level
- ☐ Goggles, gloves, and earplugs
- ☐ Sandpaper
  (in grades from fine to coarse)
- ☐ Pliers
- ☐ Allen keys
- ☐ Scraper
- ☐ Tape
- ☐ Utility knife
- ☐ Box of wall fixings
  (screws, nails, and bolts)
- ☐ Hacksaw
- ☐ Jigsaw
- ☐ Wall tester

Rex's Room ♡

As soon as we moved into Pickle Cottage, I knew I needed to start on the kids' rooms to get them settled and comfy. I wanted to do Rex's room in the most economical way to save money.

I wanted to create a room that Rex loves spending time in, a space that feels fun and exciting, where he can hang out with his brothers, cousins and friends.

The room didn't need lots of work or any expert tradespeople to be called in. Everything was already there for me to get started on, like the perfectly good fitted wardrobes that just needed upcycling.

The first thing I did in Rex's room was paint the existing fireplace. Once that was done I knew I had a colour theme for the room that we would both love. I used black, white, and grey for the colour palette, and pandas, which Rex adores, as the motif to bring it all together. I am so proud of this room. I love tidying it after Rex has made a massive mess; although, at some stage, I hope that he will learn to love tidying just as much as me. (Wishful thinking!)

I used pandas as the motif for the room!

How to

FIND A THEME FOR YOUR ROOM

When you first enter a room, it is always worth asking yourself if there is anything already there that you like and that you can use for the room's theme.

After the Blue Loo, which I themed around the beautiful enamel loo and sink, I tackled Rex's room. There was a big fireplace on one wall. It was green, with floral tiles, and really ugly but in some ways beautiful at the same time, if that makes any sense. I knew I wanted to paint it and had to be brave with it. It was tiled, gorgeous, and old and I thought: 'You know what? I have to go for it or I'm going to convince myself that it's too nice to change.' I knew I would paint it, which would mean that if we ever wanted to go back to the original colour, we could. It felt like a great way of preserving something that wasn't quite right for our family at this particular time.

I wanted to make it more neutral and needed dark colours to cover what was there, so I painted the woodwork black and the tiles grey. As soon as I had done the fireplace I knew I wanted the room to have a monochrome feel, using greys, blacks, and whites, with pops of colour using lights and other sensory stuff. It also meant I could incorporate pandas, zebras, and bears – all of Rex's favourite animals. Without overthinking it, suddenly the room theme had all come together!

If there isn't an obvious or immediate theme when you are planning a room, think about the things that make you smile, whether it is finding inspiration in the walks that you go on, in memories of things like past holidays, in family or friends whose homes you adore... it doesn't necessarily have to come from the project that you are starting from. If it does, it is a bigger bonus!

Sanding a
Wooden Floor

Hero task

There was an old green carpet on the floor in Rex's room. When we pulled it up, there were loads of disgusting and dirty planks underneath, but I knew we could bring them up well if we sanded them down. I have a hand sander, so I had a go in one corner and I saw the pine boards underneath and I knew it would be so nice if it was done properly. My excitement about what I could achieve with a larger industrial sander was not normal! It blew my mind.

I sent Joe off to pick up Sandy the sander, which we rented from a tool-hire place. He was fuming but I couldn't wait to get started. It cost £35 for the day and it did not take a day to complete the entire floor. Sandy was totally worth every penny and more! We could've done the whole of our upstairs for that if we'd been prepared, were ready to go, and put the effort in. Whenever I hire any big tools like this, I will tell the hire shop people what I am sanding – they will attach the right sandpaper for the job. There are different grades from coarse to fine, so they will be able to tell you what is best for whatever you are sanding and fit the sandpaper for you.

I know it can feel daunting but it was really simple – it is totally possible to achieve a professional result even as a beginner DIY-er.

- **Prepare the room** by removing everything from the floor, including any old floor covering, as you need a completely clear surface. Give the floor a vacuum or clean. Check for any nails that are sticking up and whack them in with a hammer or pull them out. There can be pipes in the cavity space below floorboards, so don't do any new nailing without checking for them first.

- **Replace any broken floorboards** that are split or rotting. I go to my local timber merchant to source reclaimed wooden boards, which I stain to match the existing colour.

- **Fill any chips, holes, cracks and gaps in the wood** to stop any draughts. I genuinely didn't need to do anything to the floorboards in Rex's room as there were no faults or gaps in the wood. If the gaps between boards are wide, there are different ways of filling them. Thinner gaps can be filled with papier mâché (a paper and glue mix) and be left to dry. Larger gaps can be filled with long pieces of cut wood. You need to find or cut pieces to the right size to fill the gap. Spread wood glue along the sides of the insert and knock the piece into position using another bit of wood. It can be hard to find the right size pieces to fill some gaps, so you may need to use papier mâché as well. Leave to dry.

- **Take down the curtains or blind** from the window as sanding creates an enormous amount of dust. Close the window and all the doors.

- **Cover any electrical sockets** with masking tape.

- **Make sure you have enough space** to manoeuvre your sander. Sandy was pretty wide at the bottom.

- **Get properly kitted out.** Sanding is noisy; I didn't have any noise-cancelling headphones, so I used the boys' PlayStation headset (complete with goggles and mask). I looked like a total babe!

- **Sand diagonally across the floorboards** to start. Doing this will quickly take off the worn top surface of the wood and level the floorboards. They will be very rough at this point though, but don't panic – they will get another sanding. Keep the power cable off the floor to make sure you don't run over it – I dangled it over my shoulder like a handbag.

- **Next, sand along the length of the floorboards.** Experts say to go with the grain because it leaves fewer scratches but it worked better for me going against the grain. You don't need to push the sander along as it moves by itself, but you do need to hold it back to make

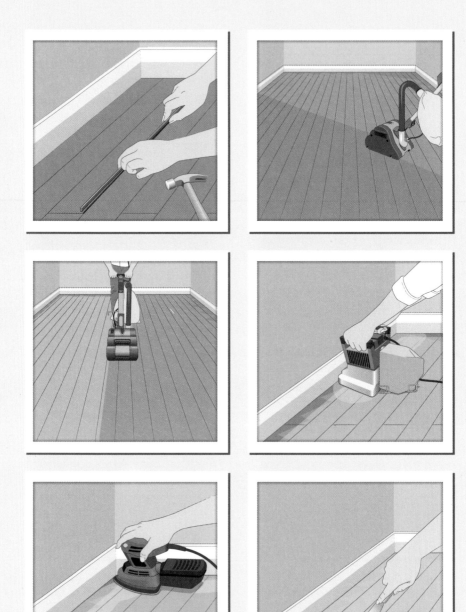

sure it doesn't run off. (Come back, Sandy!) Make sure the sander moves in a slow, steady, and straight line. And don't let it sit too long in one place because it will leave a divot if you keep sanding the same spot. Turn it on, do one line, then turn it off before doing another, so you don't damage the boards.

🐾 **Use a smaller sander or hand sander** to get into the edges and corners where the sanding belt of the larger sander cannot reach.

🐾 **Vacuum or mop the floor** to get rid of any dust. We hired an industrial vacuum for this messy job (see page 179). If you mop, leave the floor to dry.

🐾 **Seal the floorboards** using a clear wood varnish or wood stain. You can do this with a varnish floor pad or a paintbrush. The floor will need to be perfectly clean before you start, with any holes filled. Make sure you apply the sealant or stain thinly according to the instructions.

🐾 **Start at one corner furthest from the door** – you don't want to varnish yourself into the corner – and follow the lines along the grain of the wood on the boards. You might want to leave it to dry and then do another coat (or two) for the best finish. Follow the instructions regarding drying time and when to put the furniture back in.

🐾 **Add a floor rug**. To make it more comfortable for Rex, we added a black-and-white diamond-patterned rug in the middle of the room that almost covers the whole floor so he can sit on it and play with his toys.

PAINTING WARDROBES

Fitted furniture is expensive, so even if what you have in the room looks a bit shit you can still make use of it. In Rex's room, the wardrobes were nice and big but I didn't like the dark brown wood. I knew I could transform them into something nicer by painting them. I used a heavy-duty chalk-based paint, so I wouldn't have to do ten coats to cover everything. I only did a couple of coats on the wardrobe and skirting and it was done. This in turn changed the look of the whole room, tying the wardrobe, walls, and fireplace together. The inside of the wardrobe is still quite dark, so eventually, I'd like to paint the inside white.

𝒱 Wipe down the woodwork with a cloth and some household cleaner to get rid of any dust.

𝒱 Remove any drawers (so you can paint them separately) and take off any handles with a screwdriver.

𝒱 Lightly hand-sand the areas you plan to paint so the paint sticks to the wood. If your wardrobe is varnished, rub a bit harder.

𝒱 Choose your paint. I chose grey for both the wardrobe and skirting. When painting over something really dark, make sure you use a paint with a higher percentage of pigment for better coverage. It does cost a bit more; I used a Frenchic Al Fresco mineral and chalk paint, in a shade called City Slicker. This is a water-based paint that is marginally more expensive than some other brands, but I used less than I would

have with a cheaper one, so I think it probably all equalled out in the end.

𝒱 Tape up any areas that need to be protected. I taped up the glass panels in Rex's wardrobe.

𝒱 Apply the first coat of paint by working thin strokes in a consistent direction with a brush. Leave to dry.

𝒱 Apply a second coat. It can take time, but I love this type of intricate painting – I find it good for the soul!

𝒱 Re-attach the handles, either the original ones or your own new ones (see page 64), to the wardrobe doors and drawers.

𝒱 Add any finshing touches – on the open shelving area of the wardrobe, I stuck super-easy self-adhesive tiles. I used the same stickers in our last house and love the look. It's a wrap!

DIFFERENT TYPES OF PAINT EXPLAINED

Paint aisles at DIY shops? Not sure if it is just me, but sometimes they look like they are stretching on forever and they can be a bit overwhelming. In order to make sure the paint stays on your furniture or wall, it is really important to choose the type that works for you. It can be confusing, I get it, but there are two main types of paint: Water-based and oil-based.

Water-based paint, which is sometimes called emulsion, is mostly used for walls and ceilings and can cover large areas with a roller quite easily. It dries quickly, and cleaning it is also fairly easy. Oil-based paint is more durable than water-based, but drying and curing (when it becomes fully hardened) takes longer. It comes in either a gloss or a satin/eggshell finish and it is sometimes better for items like doors, floors, or busy areas like a hallway that have a lot of traffic! Within these categories, there are different options (matt emulsion, vinyl emulsion, eggshell, satin, gloss, etc.) I will always ask if I am not sure exactly what I need and I often buy some and just see if I like working with it. If I'm not sure what type is most suitable for what I want, and I plan to use it in a big area, this would be an example of when I would buy a sample paint pot. (Always use up your tester pots for upcycling projects, like the chest of drawers that I painted for Rose's nursery, see page 176.)

There are other products, including primer, that can help get a fantastic look. This is applied the same way as paint but you put it on beforehand to help the paint stick and it will seal and protect the surface. For completely new surfaces – say new skirting boards – primer is a must, but when you are painting over previously painted surfaces with a similar or darker colour, you can skip this bit! Often you can buy a primer/undercoat or paint all-in-one solution that does all the work for you. Easy!

Creating a Feature Wall

Hero task

I bought 10-litre buckets of Dulux white matt emulsion and painted the whole room white before I figured out what I would do next. It gives me a really good base to work with and then I think, 'Right, what do I want to do with this room?' I decided to do a sectioned wall and make a feature out of it. I wanted to make it funky and different.

❡ **Mark out your design**. You can do anything you want, but dividing a wall into three sections is thought to look best. I decided to divide the wall with diagonal lines from each top corner. I ended the right-hand line where the diagonals crossed in the middle and extended the left-hand diagonal to the bottom corner. This gave me three different-sized triangular shapes. I planned to leave the top triangle white and decorate it with stickers, then paint each lower triangle in a different shade of grey.

❡ **Choose your colours** – I used Frenchic Al Fresco City Slicker, again, for one section and then just mixed some black paint with white paint that I already had to make the darker shade of grey. Mixing colours you already have can save loads of money and stop you wasting any left-over paint.

❡ **Mask off the different areas** using Frog Tape – this is a brand designed for masking off when decorating. Tape your lines so they meet in the middle. If you want everything exact, it is worth using a laser spirit level (see page 174) for exact diagonal lines that are perfectly straight across the whole wall. I just taped lines across my wall, stood back to take a look and then readjusted the tape until I was happy with each line. It took me a while to work out what looked best. I think it is worth spending a bit of time on this part to make sure it is just right for you.

❡ **Paint the first masked-off area**. I started with the triangle in the lower lefthand corner and painted it in the lighter grey shade. I recommend using a paintbrush to carefully paint one line halfway over the Frog Tape

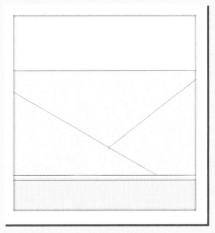

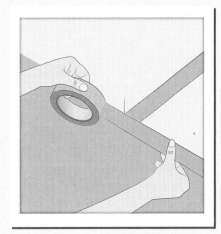

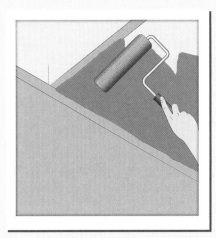

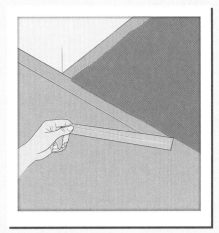

and then leave it to dry. This creates a seal between the tape and wall, leading to a cleaner finish when you peel off the tape. I didn't do this at first and the paint bled into the tape. Remove the tape from that section.

🖤 **Paint the second area** once the first is dry. Reposition a clean length of tape along the edge of the first

area, just covering the paint. I didn't reposition the tape in Rex's room so I was left with a gap between the two triangles, which needed to be filled in.

🖤 **Add wall stickers to one section**. The animal wall stickers I used came from Amazon. They peel on and off really easily. I just dotted them around, whacking them on anywhere!

WHY NOT WALLPAPER?

I haven't used wallpaper in Pickle Cottage because I like the look of the painted walls. I think you have to be so sure about wallpaper because it is quite expensive and it takes more time to hang than slapping some paint on. It's also quite particular in terms of style. I will use wallpaper if there is quite a large space and I want to change up one of the walls or make it feel a bit different. There are a lot of so-called 'rules' with wallpapering and sometimes it is nice to follow them, but it bugs me when people say, 'just pick out one wall and paper that'. If you like a busy wallpaper and you want it on every wall, you should do it. If you don't like it, you don't have to keep it there, but give it a go anyway.

At Pickle Cottage, I haven't had a massive room to do, where I have felt that it needs to be different and wallpaper might have been the answer. I considered it for Rex's room, but then I found wall stickers and I felt that they would be easier and fun, and it didn't have to be perfect. I have also been experimenting with different paint methods, like the feature wall in this room. With that, I hoped to create some sort of interest without needing to wallpaper. This is cheaper and is something else that no one else will have, so it feels really unique. I felt creative in a different way.

My top wallpapering tips would be:

♥ Measure your walls to work out how many rolls of wallpaper you need. You can make the calculations yourself but it is a good idea to get them doublechecked by asking in the shop. I recommend getting an extra roll or two as you can always return what you don't use. It is better to have extra, so you don't need to go back to the shop.

♥ Make sure all the rolls have the same batch number so they are an exact colour match. Another reason to buy more than enough, so you don't risk not being able to get another roll from the same batch.

♥ Decide what section of the paper you want to place in the centre of the wall, depending on the pattern, which is where your eye is drawn.

♥ Start papering in the centre of the wall. I always place exactly what I want in the middle. Sometimes when I have started in a corner, I have then got to the centre and thought, 'That's not quite where I wanted it.' I would rather the sides look a bit out than the very middle of the wall.

♥ Make sure you start straight but don't go from the ceiling unless your ceiling and walls are dead straight. Don't measure to the top of the wall, but just below it. Get that one vertical line straight with a spirit or laser level, put up the paper and overlap it onto the ceiling, then cut it back afterwards. I find by doing it that way, with each wallpaper strip, it is easy to make sure the pattern matches.

- Get out your caulk! When you have finished, don't be afraid to caulk along the top and bottom of the paper. Sometimes people leave it a bit unfinished and wonder what to do. My answer to that? Caulk, baby! This also stops dirt from gathering

and leaves a clean and smooth finish. I think it helps wallpaper last longer as it stops the corners from lifting away from the wall.

- If you are left with off-cuts, use them. If you buy wallpaper, it's because you love the design, so use the cuttings for other stuff like drawer liners or to line a craft box. You can use it for anything – even to wrap a present!

- Always keep a spare roll of any wallpaper just in case the pattern is later discontinued and you need to do any patch-ups.

USE THE LIGHTING FIXTURES

I have two sets of lights in Rex's room. The cute cloud-shaped lights on the wall above his bed are from IKEA – they were so, so cheap and are gorgeous. I have a flat light on the other wall. Flat lights are ideal for walls or ceiling spaces where the ceiling is low or you are trying to save space – I also have one in my blue loo.

My tip would always be: where there are existing attachments with fittings, be sure to use them and stick with the same lighting spot. You can change the light, but leave the fittings where they are. It is easier to make do with what you've got and make a feature of those lights.

I love to make lights more of a fun, interactive play feature. I bought Rex some hexagonal touch lights that he is obsessed with. I was a bit gutted they were not multicoloured (like the pictures suggested) but he was still very happy with them. Each of the lights, which are USB-charged, can be moved individually to make letters, numbers, or shapes, like a heart or anything really. He can move them around as he likes! I also bought a couple of light-up stars for the wall by his bed.

Panda Drawer Handles

I was looking for panda handles forever. I found plenty but they were awful.
It is so hard when you know exactly what you are looking for and can't find it!
Rex had these plastic panda toys from Fenwick – they were £3.50 for six.
I thought they would look amazing as handles and I searched high and low
for something like it but they just didn't exist. So I used the toys to make my
own unique panda handles. The simplest things can make all the difference!
Rex is obsessed with them – he talks to them and plays with them all the time.

| STEP 1 | STEP 2 | STEP 3 | STEP 4 |

♥ **DRILL A HOLE** in the back of the panda toy, or whatever you are using for
your handle, but make it shallow so you don't go through to the other side.

♥ **MAKE A LARGER HOLE** in the drawer front, if you need to, unless you
are reusing the screw from the original handle.

♥ **THREAD THE SCREW** through the drawer from the inside to the outside.

♥ **TWIST THE PANDA TOY** onto the screw to secure it in place. You may
need to put a rawl plug into the drilled hole or add a dab of strong glue in
there to help it stay firm and snug and make sure it doesn't fall off.

Panda Wall Display

What does your kid love? We are always at IKEA (this is genuinely one of my favourite *ever* shops and when I've not been for a while, I miss that blue and yellow flag so much!) and Rex is obsessed with the stuffed panda toys there. Every time we go, we have to buy one. He loves all animals, so I decided to do a wall display using cuddly pandas attached directly to the wall.

- ♡ **MARK ON THE WALL** where you want the stuffed toys to go.

- ♡ **DRILL HOLES IN THE WALL** using the right drill bit.

- ♡ **POP IN SOME RAWL PLUGS**, making sure these are the right ones for your wall. Walls like stud walls need rawl plugs with little arms that grip the plasterboard. I just needed normal rawl plugs for this job.

- ♡ **FIX THE TOYS TO THE WALL** using screws in the rawl plugs. The toy will spin round as you screw, so make sure you stop when it's the right way up! I carefully arranged the pandas so that the screws aren't visible when you're looking at them. Pinch any excess fabric at the back of the stuffed toy, tap a nail with a large head through the fabric into the wall.

- ♡ **PAINT A SCENE**. At first, my pandas looked like something out of 'The Human Centipede' because they were grabbing each other's bums. The kids laughed so hard about this – Leighton was like, 'One is feeling the other one's bum!'. To fix this, I painted a balloon at the top of the wall for the pandas to hold onto, to make it look a bit sweeter and more suitable for a toddler's room! You can add anything you want though.

- ♡ **ADD ANY EXTRAS**, like special wall stickers. I added a quote saying, 'The best thing to hold onto in life is each other!' (And bums – I didn't really include that bit!). I get all my labels and stickers from my sister Jemma's company, The Label Lady.

Quick fix

PAINTING A TILED FIREPLACE

The first thing I got to work on in this room was the fireplace. I knew I needed to get my big girl pants on and just have a go at changing it and making it a bit more neutral. It was an antique fireplace but wasn't particularly valuable. Part of me felt a bit sad that I was going over the flowered ceramic tiles but they didn't feel right for Rex's room. Once I had done it, it set a colour theme for the room that I kept running with. Here are instructions for how I did it:

♥ Buy the right type of paint for whatever material your fireplace is made from. I bought wood paint for the fireplace surround and tile paint to cover the tiles. I painted the hearth black, and I chose grey paint for the remaining areas, including the mantelpiece.

♥ Use heat-resistant paint or use a primer under the paint if you are going to light a fire in the fireplace. To be sure, you can use both to prevent any soot and dirt coming through to the paintwork. It goes without saying, that this fireplace in Rex's room is never going to be a working fireplace!

♥ Sand everything down using sandpaper and elbow grease, then clean the whole area to get rid of all dust and dirt.

♥ Tackle one section at a time when painting. Use masking tape to keep the edge of the painted area in a straight line. I used a brush because it was a small area, so I could be more accurate. Brushes often come in packs of four different sizes and the middle two are good sizes to start with. Find what works best for you. You may need multiple coats to make the colour stand out. I did two coats on mine. It looked quite silver to start with but came out a matt grey once it dried.

♥ Shine up any metalwork that is dull or weathered using special metal polish. I didn't do anything with the metalwork here as it was fine.

We then added some black-and-white prints – 'Little Explorer', 'Adventure', and 'Wild Child' – hanging them with Command Strips (see page 124), and I attached some cute little stuffed toy zebra heads above the fireplace. Now he gives them a little kiss every morning on his way to brush his teeth. So adorable!

Little things I love ♡

HEIGHT CHART

We love measuring our kids to track how they are growing (way too fast, if you ask me!). In his room, Rex has this cute wooden height chart in the shape of an old-fashioned school ruler that I bought from a small business called Family Rule. Joe fixed it to the wall about 10cm above the floor, so every time we measure him, we need to add that 10cm back on to Rex's height!

MAKING A CHALKBOARD ON THE WALL

I think with some blank walls you can really create a space that allows kids to be creative. I wanted the room to be really fun for Rex and be somewhere that he loved, with the right amount of storage and exciting stuff. All Rex wants to do is draw. I am not joking – getting the chance to draw on the wall is his life's work! I knew that I could buy a chalkboard but the reality is that he wants to draw on the walls. I wondered if I could make a wall for drawing so I didn't have to tell him off all the time, and he would know that that was his space.

I researched 'chalkboards', 'chalkboard paints' and 'how to build a chalkboard on the wall' and I saw that there was a specific type of paint that could go on the wall to make a chalkboard. I opted for Securit Chalkboard Paint in grey. It was £9 and easy enough to paint the original wall, plus I have some left for when it needs to be retouched.

♥ Give yourself plenty of time. I didn't realise that it would take 48 hours minimum for the paint to dry and that I would have to do two coats so, essentially, it's a four-day project, whether you like it or not.

♥ Open the windows! In general, chalkboard paint is really runny and smelly. While I was painting, I made sure Rex was not in the room. Once I had finished, I let it air out for a week until he slept in there again. There was no warning on the tin, but it just didn't smell good to me. That's my heads up.

♥ Mark out the area you want to paint, masking it off with tape as usual.

♥ Start painting. Because the paint was so runny, it was not easy to keep it inside the tape lines. I had to catch the dripping paint to stop it running all over the floor. Even though I was careful and tried to load the brush with as little paint as possible, it still ran and the lines didn't look that straight. This annoyed me, so I decided to add a border.

♥ Add a border. I used lengths of skirting, which was some leftover bits from the boys' room. I measured the perimeter of the painted area and cut the skirting to the right lengths. Then I cut the ends at 45-degree angles and framed the entire thing using my favourite adhesive, No More Nails.

♥ Add a shelf. In the bottom corner of the chalkboard I put a floating shelf, like the ones in the Blue Loo. It saved me cutting a corner of wood so it was way easier, and it is somewhere Rex can put his chalks and chalkboard rubber.

♥ Use sealant around the area when it is completely dry and tidy it up.

♥ Add some stick-on pen holders. Mine came from eBay, and this is where Rex puts his chalks.

How to

GET CREATIVE WITH STORAGE

Let's face it: kids have loads of stuff. Toys, cars, arts and crafts stuff, books, more toys... sometimes I feel like I am wading through a jungle of their things. Don't fret! I don't think they can ever have too much storage and I think it is possible to have kids and a tidy house. Making clever use of storage in kids' rooms totally makes sense and if you have ever trodden on some LEGO or a bit of plastic in the dark, you will understand where I am coming from here.

The first bed I bought for Rex was a massive bunk bed which was gigantic and too big for the room, so Leighton got that one instead (I'll talk more about why I think this is a great piece of furniture later). I decided to buy Rex a more compact bed but made sure it had space underneath for loads of storage baskets to hide away his things. This is where we put the stuff he doesn't play with all the time, like some of his cuddly toys and his Hot Wheels tracks that he doesn't have out every day. I also put his books in a box so, at bedtime, he can pull it out and choose one as his bedtime story.

I fitted a panda shelf from HomeZone that sits on one wall, and some IKEA Kallax units that go under the windows. I think IKEA storage for kids is the best; you know it will get drawn and climbed on, so it is best to buy reasonably priced units. Under windows is always a great spot for storage and avoids the area being 'dead space' – you can make walls work hard and this type of storage in a kid's room is ideal if you ask me. These units came with little attachments so you can fix them straight to the wall. If you buy these types of units, don't be afraid to get them out of the box and just get on with securing them to the wall because they are much easier than they look, I promise. If you Google 'IKEA Kallax hacks', there are loads of ideas on the Internet on how to make these units look good and also make them a great storage option for practically anything.

Then I bought some trays and labelled them up with separate names for stuff: Trains, drawing, dinosaurs, vegetables, cooking, and painting. This is the stuff that he plays with all the time.

I actually love it when his room is a mess and I can have the satisfaction of tidying everything away into the right place, but I do want him to learn to put things back in the right place eventually! If I was going to do it again, I would make the labels have lower-case letters rather than capital letters, so now that Rex is learning to read and write, he could read them a bit more easily.

ROTATE YOUR TOYS

We only put some of Rex's toys out and store the rest in the loft. After a few months when he is bored with what he has been playing with and starts asking for new toys, we bring them back out and it feels like a whole new set of toys! Doing this with kids just keeps their play fresh and interesting without having to spend loads of money on new stuff.

WHAT TO KEEP AND WHAT TO GET RID OF?

Sometimes you have to make some hard decisions about what to keep and what to recycle or chuck out. You have to love your home – don't keep something because someone else tells you that you have to! In Rex's room, I decided to replace the curtains – they were so huge and heavy that they closed the room off a lot and made it feel boxed in, and really dark.

I sent the curtains off to somewhere that uses old fabrics to make kids' clothes. The other curtains in the house got very dirty when we were sanding and were just generally old and very worn, so we sent them to just be recycled. When all the rooms are done, I plan to buy all the curtains for all the rooms that need them in one go to save some money. By bulk buying, you will always bring the cost down. Curtains, blinds and shutters really can add up, so this is how I plan to do it. Luckily the cottage is not overlooked by anyone else and so it doesn't matter if we don't have anything covering all the windows for a while.

TRUST THE INSTRUCTIONS

In Rex's room, I have a colourful sensory bubble display and it is quite big. Looking at it, you would worry it would be hard to put up but I made sure I read carefully what I needed to do. I put the base on, filled it with water and secured the top. It was pretty much straightforward – as long as I was following the right instructions! It is so pretty, with different streams of coloured bubbles running through it, especially when it is dark, and Rex loves it. Being allowed to draw on the chalkboard in his bedroom has channelled all of Rex's creativity into this one space and stopped him drawing on other walls in the cottage. Rather than being something naughty, he knows that drawing on walls is now allowed (although only in this one place) and, as it doesn't get my attention in the same way any longer, his overall behaviour has improved.

Little things I love ♡

HAND SANDER

I've had a hand sander forever. These tools, which are sometimes called palm sanders, are so easy to use and are ideal for tackling smaller areas. Even if you have a table that you want to upcycle, sanding it down manually can take so much effort. Just run your electric hand sander up and down and it changes everything! It is also great for getting into corners and edges of bigger areas.

I would always advise going in on the lowest power level first and getting used to it before going up the levels. Don't press down too hard on the sander: remember that slow and steady wins this race!

How to

FIND INSPIRATION WHEN SHOPPING

I think shopping online is great but sometimes you can go round and round in circles looking on Pinterest or other channels trying to think of ideas with a million tabs open and still not feel like you've found what you want.

You just can't beat a trip to a proper shop to get ideas. Some days after my morning cuppa, I will hop in the car and go to home stores – even though I don't plan to buy anything – and look at their displays and see how they put things together.

I will go to IKEA, Homesense, or Next Home, or wherever it might be, pop Rex and Rose in the trolley and whizz around, just to see how they have styled things. Whether it's adding bright cushions or a gallery wall to a living area, or clever lighting in a bedroom, their stylists often totally nail it. You might find an item you love but wonder how you are going to tie it into the rest of your home, so by doing this you can find new ideas.

So, say you want a really brightly coloured sofa but are wondering how it would fit into a room in your house? I would go into a sofa shop and look at the way they have tied the look of a sofa to the room: the wall colours around it, the flooring, the cushions and vases, and how they connected the different items together. Seeing things in real life gives you a better sense of how things look in a way that you can't see when you're browsing online. You can also ask questions and get a human response which is even better!

PREP TO PAINT
Checklist

- [ ] Dust sheets
- [ ] Stepladder *(if you need it)*
- [ ] Tape measure
- [ ] Masking tape
- [ ] Sandpaper
- [ ] Filler or wall putty *(if you need it)*
- [ ] Primer
- [ ] Paint
- [ ] Paintbrushes of all sizes
- [ ] Paint rollers
- [ ] Long-handled paint roller or extension pole
- [ ] Paint tray
- [ ] Caulk and cartridge gun applicator
- [ ] Knife
- [ ] Cleaning rag
- [ ] Protective gear *(mask and goggles)*

The Boys' Rooms

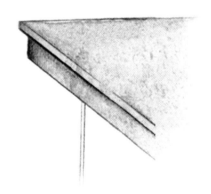

As well as getting Rex's room set up as soon as we'd moved in, I wanted to make sure Zachary and Leighton were comfy too. They now each have their own space – they are so lucky.

As I said earlier, my dad helped me by putting up a stud wall to make two rooms – one each for my older boys. When dividing up a space, it's really important that it meets building regulations, especially with regards to natural light and ventilation.

Think carefully about the size of the space, how each room will be used and if there will be enough floor space for furniture. If it's for a bedroom, think about whether you will be able to walk around the bed and have enough storage for clothes and so on. We were fortunate as it was a really big space, so there was plenty of room for all the furniture the boys wanted in each room. Their rooms are connected by a single door, which is perfect for them (they are always popping in and out of each other's rooms!) but if you are dividing a space, it is worth considering whether you need a corridor for independent access to each room.

Zachary and Leighton have never had their own rooms before; they've always shared, so it was important to me that they were involved at every step. I wanted them to have a say in how their rooms were decorated and put their stamp on it; I let them choose the colours, so it was exactly what they wanted. Zachary wanted to paint his own room so I put a dust sheet on the floor and let him get on with it – he painted the whole thing electric blue. Leighton's room is a pale blue.

They both needed fitted wardrobes. I decided to invest in some really good ones from Sharps, so they can be their forever furniture. The boys came with me to the shop to design the fitted furniture themselves. They both sat in with me and I asked them all the questions I was being asked. I wanted them to say what they wanted, so they felt like they had ownership. The boys are delighted with their wardrobes. They both have loads of shelving for their special bits and bobs.

We had a lot of outside help with their bedrooms. As well as building the stud wall and fitted furniture (which includes desk space), Dad helped with all the wiring for Leighton's LED lights on his wall (see page 91). We also had flooring fitted. I love the fact that my dad helped to build the wall and the boys were so excited to see what he was doing. It was like his house-warming gift to them! These were the bedrooms that took the longest from start to finish, but it was so worth it.

The first night their rooms were finished, we all had sleepovers in there, which they loved. It was like they were welcoming me into their house – even though it was just their bedrooms! I'm not going to lie, I didn't get the best night's sleep, but it is such a lovely memory. The boys absolutely love their rooms (and so do I!). I hope they make the best memories there.

Little things I love ♡

MULTI-PURPOSE FURNITURE

Leighton is at that age where it is sleepover central, so having a bunk bed is really important to him, whereas Zach is like, 'I don't want another sleepover Mum!' I love Leighton's bed because it has shelving and bits all integrated into it and it is a brilliant use of space.

He inherited the bunk bed as it was originally bought for Rex; it was massive – far too big for Rex's room. My advice is to always make sure the furniture you are buying fits the space before you order it! In the end it worked out OK because Leighton just came in and said, 'I want that bed,' so I was relieved that I didn't have to take it back. He's very happy with it and it has loads of space for his stuff – and his friends!

How to

PUT UP FLAT-PACK FURNITURE

Flat-pack furniture can go from the easiest thing in the world – like an IKEA Kallax unit, where you pop it together and Bob's your uncle, the job is done in about ten minutes – to something like Leighton's bed. Once I realised it was never going to fit in Rex's room and it was already half-built, I made Joe and my brother-in-law carry it into Leighton's room. It was a beast. I'm not going to lie, at one point my eye was twitching like mad when I was putting it together. There was no way I was taking that apart!

♥ Before buying the furniture, always make sure you have enough space for it. (Learn from MY mistakes!)

♥ Preparation is really important. Create enough space to work in: so, make sure the area is clear of anything else. The best thing you can do at the start is to lay out all the parts. Sometimes they come with stickers on, so an item or group of items will say 'A', or 'B', so lay these in the right order, as well as all the tools you might need, onto the floor. This will save a lot of time.

♥ Sometimes it's not clear what goes where, so work out which screws are for which piece. Many of these vary in size only slightly, so measure them up against each other, or the instructions, to make sure you have the right ones. As you're unpacking everything, be careful not to scratch it.

- Always have a power tool handy. The furniture will probably come with an Allen key or instructions to use a screwdriver, but having to screw in manually can bust your hands. Also, you can't tighten screws as well as you can with a power tool. I also use my drill as a screwdriver (more on this later – see page 84).

- Follow the instructions carefully. Don't scrimp on this bit: read them from beginning to end before starting so you've got a rough idea of what you need to do. If you don't do this, I think it is really easy to make mistakes that just mess everything else up.

- Take your time. I love jobs that take five minutes but putting up flat-pack furniture is not one of those. If you need to, take a break. I find that if I rush, I am more likely to make mistakes. You don't want to have to re-do the whole thing because you have missed a step.

- Get help. Sometimes two hands are better than one, and I get Joe or my dad to help out if I need someone to hold something in place whilst I screw it in or if the furniture is really heavy.

- Once you've done it, check you have used all the parts. Sometimes there will be the odd spare screw or small item, so don't panic, but all the main parts should now be used.

- Keep the Allen key and assembly instructions somewhere safe just in case you need to take apart the furniture in the future, such as when the item is sold or recycled because your kid has outgrown it or needs to be packed down when moving house.

USE A DRILL

Don't be scared of power tools! I love my drill. I know it can seem intimidating and I had all those feelings when I started using it too. I remember when Dad got me a drill for the first time and it was all mine. I don't think you should ever not bother with a drill. As far as I am concerned, it is essential for most DIY jobs. I think the best ones are the simpler ones – cordless, easy to use, and that can do a variety of stuff.

You can use a drill for:

❤ Making a hole in a material like wood, stone or metal, etc. by using a drill and a drill bit. Most drills have a normal rotating action and also a hammer drilling action; this gives the drill more power, as the drill bit goes in with a punching force whilst also going round. You may need this for drilling through a tougher material, like concrete. Don't use a hammer drill on a stud wall as it will make a MASSIVE hole.

❤ You can also use many drills for driving a screw into material, using the correct bit. When you use an ordinary screwdriver, it can take ages, you get hand cramps, and it's boring. With this, you can basically turn your drill into a power screwdriver! It's much quicker and easier, trust me.

MY TOP DRILL TIPS

Ѷ Always make sure you check for hidden pipes and cables first. Avoid areas directly above and below switches and sockets.

Ѷ Choose the right drill bit for the job (see page 43). If it's the wrong one, the material you are drilling into could crack or break. You attach each drill bit by loosening the chuck (the circular section at the end of the drill) with a special key and by inserting the bit and then re-tightening the chuck so it is secure.

Ѷ Make sure whatever you are drilling is stable and secure – and that you are, too. You don't want to be wobbling around on the top of a ladder!

Ѷ Hold the drill at a right angle to whatever you are drilling, go steadily, and pull the drill back out again every few seconds to let the drilled material fall out and not get stuck. Every drill has a trigger and like any type of trigger, the harder you squeeze, the harder it goes. It is always a good idea to have a fully charged battery because this can affect the drill's speed.

Ѷ Go cordless! My drill is a basic one from IKEA and is battery operated, rather than mains operated. The bottom basically comes off and charges and then plugs back in. This is much more convenient to use – I love a cordless tool!

Ѷ Always make sure you are not distracted. Whenever I am doing my DIY I will always make sure Joe is in charge of the kids, so no one is shouting, 'Muuuuum!' mid drilling session. I also put my phone to one side, so I can completely focus on the job in hand.

Ѷ If I am quickly drilling a single hole into a wall, when hanging a picture, for example, then I stick an open envelope to the wall with masking tape just underneath the drilled hole to catch any falling debris. This means less mess to vacuum up once you're done.

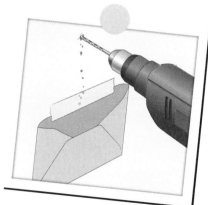

Little things I love ♡

WALL-MOUNTED LED LIGHTS

Leighton just loves the LED lights on his wall and so do I! They are so colourful and fun. He always wants to save up his pocket money and buy more – he collects them. The ones in his room are from Amazon and they are powdered by USB cables that plug into a box in his room, so he can switch them on and off.

Before we got the plasterer in, we got an electrician to make sure there were enough USB sockets for the lights to run off and chase the sockets through the wall (that is, inset the boxes into the wall), so they did not need to be on the outside, and the whole area looked neat.

Quick fix

SPRAY-PAINTING SPOTLIGHT FITTINGS

Do you have lights in your home where the fixture is OK but you hate the colour? The spotlights in the boys' rooms were an odd colour and looked really old, so I decided to take the fittings out and spray-paint them white so they blended in with the rest of the ceiling. It's amazing what spray paint can do! It comes in an aerosol can with a nozzle and is so easy to apply.

- Make sure that the power is fully turned off.

- Standing on a step ladder, remove the bulb and carefully pull the light surrounds from the ceiling – my ones popped out really easily.

- If they are dusty or greasy, wash them first. Make sure you don't use anything with harsh chemicals, as this could affect the way the paint sticks to them. Allow them to dry.

- Lay down an old sheet or newspaper before painting indoors. I painted mine outdoors as it was a warm, dry day. When working outdoors, beware of flying insects as they are attracted to wet paint, which does not result in a good look!

- To paint the fittings, simply press the spray can nozzle and go. Make sure you stay a good distance from the lights (around 20 cm) so the coverage is even. I used an all-in-one primer, paint, and topcoat spray – there are loads of these types of paints available for use inside and outside. I also chose white as the ceiling is white, but you can spray-paint light fittings in any colour. The ones in Rose's room are a muted gold, which I love.

- Paint one side and leave the fittings to dry, then turn them over and paint the other side. Repeat on either side if needed.

- Once completely dry, put the fitting and bulb back in and turn on!

I painted these light fittings before I bought my paint sprayer, which is very cool and I love it (see page 243). They are designed for doing bigger jobs, like painting kitchen units and other large bits of furniture, but if I had owned the paint sprayer then I would have totally tried it on these light fittings. It makes painting much quicker and gives a much more even finish than hand-painting.

WHERE TO STORE THINGS

When it came to storage in the boys' rooms, the top drawers nearest the desk will always be the ones full of stationery, pencils, and the bits and bobs they need to do their schoolwork. Leighton has got some colourful storage boxes for his LEGO that look great, so they live on top of his drawers.

I always put their toys in the bottom drawers because if they're playing on the floor, they'll want to be close to their toys. The drawers next to the wardrobe I use for underwear.

I try to store the boys' clothing in clear sections. The problem we had when we first moved into Pickle Cottage was the boys kept getting told off at school for not having the right stuff with them because the house was all over the place. Once they had their new furniture and drawers, they knew exactly where stuff was – and they just continue with the system I have in place. Leighton is particularly good at this. He really takes it on board and loves to organise his stuff. They don't lose anything, it is less effort for me, and I don't end up hunting high and low every morning or arguing with them. Now I get to enjoy my mornings a lot more.

GO FOR THE DOUBLE

We were lucky enough to design our own wardrobes for the boys and it was so much fun! I love everything about these wardrobes, including the integrated lighting and all the different compartments. One thing I would say is this: if you are choosing or designing wardrobes for kids, I would always advise you to go for double hanging, with two lots of rails, one below the other. This is particularly if you have boys – they don't have any long flowing dresses and you will get double the amount of hanging space for the stuff they use a lot like t-shirts and uniforms.

How to

REMOVE OLD SKIRTING BOARDS

I think skirting boards are so important to make a room look neatly framed and pretty. Most rooms have existing skirting boards and I would always try and use what I have before buying new. Unusually, the boys' space did not have skirting already in place, but if you want to remove skirting, here is this step, in case you need it.

There are many reasons why you might want to remove old skirting. These boards are there to protect the walls and sometimes they are just so old and knackered that you will want to replace them. It's normal for cables to run along behind the skirting, and sometimes you may need to get at them. Always be very careful of the wiring behind as you attempt to take off old skirting boards.

♥ If there is sealant or caulk along the top of the skirting, take a Stanley knife and run it between the skirting and the wall. If you don't want to redecorate, it's really important to be particularly careful not to damage the paint (and save yourself another job!).

♥ The next step is to loosen the skirting, so you can pull it away from the wall. Most skirting will either be glued or nailed in. Take a chisel and knock it gently with a hammer between the wall and the skirting. Continue this action at a few points along the skirting board and hopefully this will be enough to loosen the skirting.

♥ Use a crowbar to pull away the skirting, ideally placing a block of thin wood between the crowbar and the wall to protect the wall.

♥ If there are nails remaining in the wood or the wall, use pliers to take these out.

How to

ORGANISE GAMING EQUIPMENT

As much as it pains me to say so, my boys are obsessed with gaming and their PlayStations. Leighton is really tidy and hates all the mess and wires, so we worked out ways to make it all a bit tidier.

We bought Leighton a Sonic the Hedgehog control holder, so he knows exactly where the controller is. Then, we got a wire tube that groups all the wires and cables together. Then we made a hole in his desk to feed the wires through, so they are not all over his desk. The whole space is much clearer and he is happier with it.

If you have cables that you don't use all the time, make sure you make space for them in a drawer and use cable dividers. There are loads of different styles; we like the ones that you can fix into drawers which have clip holders that are suitable for all types of cables.

THE BOYS' KITCHENETTE

There was a lovely cute kitchen area by the boys' bedrooms. There was no hob, microwave or fridge but just some units and a sink. We were never going to build them a whole kitchen in that space because we were saving for our family kitchen, but I wanted to make it nice and to renovate it for them. I thought it might help them gain some independence, so they can get their own breakfast in the mornings and help themselves to snacks. I also put a little cleaning box in there – if they don't want to live in a pigsty, then they have to clean it! They do get it out now and again and sort their lives out. With this space, they have a little taste of freedom.

PAINTING UNITS AND CHANGING HANDLES

First of all, I painted the kitchenette units in a navy-blue vinyl matt emulsion to revive them; it took three coats of paint to cover each door. The paint I used was 'Admiral' from Wickes. Then, I put on some Goldenwarm kitchen door handles from Amazon. I just thought that gold went so well with the dark blue. Then I put up a little floating shelf high in the corner.

SPRAY-PAINTING A SINK

Next, I spray-painted the sink. It was all scratched up and not very nice, but I didn't want to buy a whole new sink, so I decided to revive it. I had a look on Google and loads of people had spray-painted their sinks. If you are renovating and doing a job like this, I would advise doing this part of it first, but I was waiting for Joe to help me as I was heavily pregnant, so I'd stopped using spray paint. I did everything else and left this job until last.

I read a lot about how you should try not to spray the inside of the bowl but I needed to do this one because it looked so bad. So far, the paint has lasted fine. I may need to re-do it at some point but it didn't cost much to do, so I'm not worried. Currently, it looks like a new sink!

- Scrub the sink really well with a Brillo pad to get rid of all the dirt and grime.

- Prime the area first. Joe used a spray primer to help get a better finish. I don't always do this but I knew that this job would need it.

- Get spraying. We used an epoxy waterproof white spray paint called Deco Color Epoxy Keramik and it took two cans to cover it.

- Seal the area with a special sealant designed for sinks. We used a spray sealer on ours.

COVERING A SURFACE IN VINYL

When I decorated my last house, I only did stuff that was cost-effective as we knew we wouldn't be there forever. One of the things I did was cover the utility room cupboards and worktops in self-adhesive vinyl, which is durable, waterproof and doesn't peel. It changed the whole room for about £25 and made me so happy. I used the same type of vinyl on the worktops in the boys' kitchenette.

❦ Take down any curtains, clear the surfaces, and remove any old vinyl.

❦ Measure your surfaces and jot the measurements down. Get a roll the width of your surface, if possible. Make sure you buy enough – I always buy an extra one – so for this project, I was left with a spare one. The vinyl we used for this kitchen area was from Amazon and is called Hode Marble.

❦ Make sure the surface is spotlessly clean, then dampen it slightly.

❦ Start laying the vinyl down, peeling off the backing as you go. There is a specific tool you can use, but I use anything hard or straight to smooth it out into the wall and sides – it's a bit like covering a school book! For this job, I used a flat scraping tool. Even a piece of scrap wood that is completely flat would be fine. It's not as complicated as it looks! Prick any air bubbles with a pin and use a hairdryer to smooth the vinyl out.

❦ Trim any excess away at the edges or tuck it under, if there is space. If you are unhappy with anything, peel the vinyl back and have another go.

❦ Seal the edges of the vinyl by running a line of silicone sealant or caulk along the wall or any joins (see page 114).

HEAD OUTDOORS WHEN YOU CAN

Anything you can saw, cut, spray or paint outdoors, do it outside. Especially if it's messy, dusty, or smells of fumes – or you are pregnant! Whether I am pregnant or not, I find it makes for a nicer experience and paint dries more quickly out in the sun. If I am painting, I lay down old sheets and paint on them. For sawing stuff, I use a special workbench with clamps and always do it outside in fine weather, or in one of our sheds if the weather is bad.

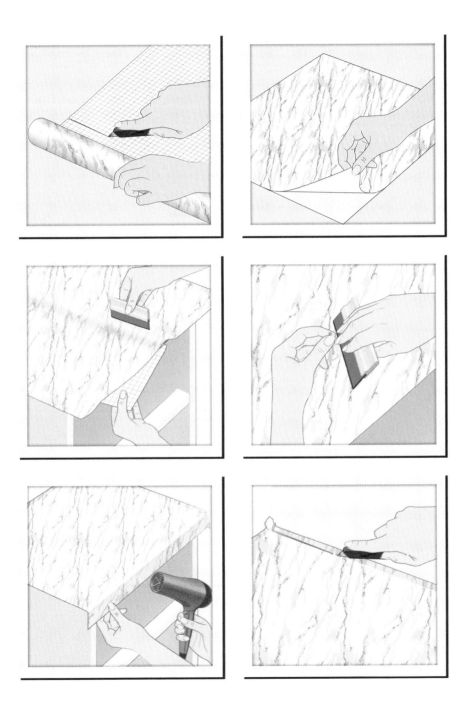

The Conservatory

Some of my most favourite memories of Pickle Cottage so far are of being in the conservatory. I just love the wide expanses of glass. It's a lovely place to sit in the evening and watch the sunset.

When we moved into Pickle Cottage, it was a really cold March – spring was taking ages to get started. Probably like the rest of us in early 2021, it was not quite sure whether it was coming or going!

The garden surrounding the cottage is beautiful but, at that time of the year, just coming out of winter, everything looked a bit dead. There were no leaves on the trees and no bulbs had sprouted yet. Over the weeks that followed, it was magical to watch the entire garden, the trees, the shrubs, and the flowers, come to life at different times. When I come down to the conservatory each morning and look out over the garden, I never quite know what is going to be out there.

About a month after we moved in, I went into the garden one day and there was an entire section of the garden where a little sea of bluebells had popped up overnight. It made me so emotional, like it was Christmas morning or something. It was so pretty and it really reminded me of being a kid. The colour was just stunning! I thought, 'I want a room like the bluebells. I want a purple room or a lilac room.' So I got busy painting and doing up the conservatory.

I love the colour and texture of the oak floor we had laid in our conservatory, with its brown and cream tones. It makes me feel all warm inside. There are so many ways to bring different textures to a room. Adding greenery and flowers is one of my favourites, but something as simple as adding a rug with a high pile or fringing can transform the feeling of a room and make it seem cosier. Embracing the less-than-perfect-parts of a room also creates some texture. So my wall rose isn't perfect but that doesn't matter – to me, this just adds character and makes it unique!

PAINTING WALLS

I think a lick of fresh paint can make a massive difference to a room. For the conservatory, I knew I wanted a lilac colour, so I went to Wickes to look for purple paint. They stocked two different purples, one dark and one light, and so I went for the lighter one.

When I paint a large space, like a wall, I literally take a large paintbrush or paint roller and I paint. I don't overthink it. I just slap the paint on and if I don't like what I have just done, I simply go over it. I think it is much easier to get an even, smooth finish with a microfibre paint roller with a short pile – I hate those massive, fluffy ones. While they are the best for textured surfaces, they leave loads of marks behind on a smooth wall. I really like a straightforward, easy-to-clean, microfibre roller. I also prefer the smaller ones: it takes a little bit longer but I feel I can get in places with them that I can't with a larger roller.

❦ Choose your paint. There are different types of paint (see page 59) but if you are unsure what you need, just ask the staff at the DIY store for advice.

❦ Prepare your walls. Some people clean the areas or sand them down first but, if the walls are in good shape, I don't always bother! Start by taking a good look at your walls. If you have any holes in the plasterwork, you will need to fill them carefully first (see page 217). Ensure they are flat after filling, and leave them to dry. Tackle any rough plaster

or peeling paintwork with sandpaper. It is always better to have a flat and even surface to paint on. If your walls are dirty or dusty, you may also want to give them a wash using sugar soap (see page 33), or mild detergent and water, and a damp sponge, making sure you don't get water in any lights or plug sockets. Leave the wall to dry thoroughly.

❦ When painting straight lines, if you don't have a steady hand, run masking tape around the windows, doors and any built-in furniture. I always cover the skirting boards

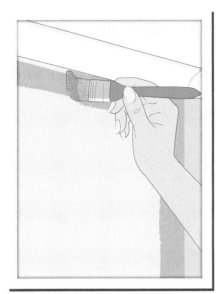

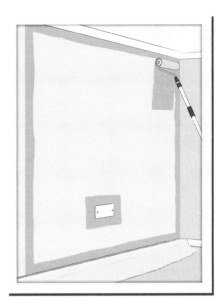

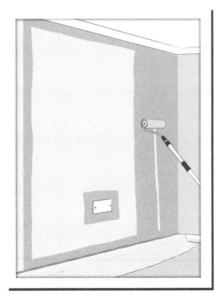

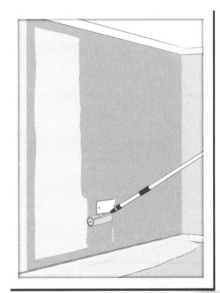

with masking tape to stop them getting splattered with any spots from my paint roller. Rather than taping around electrical sockets and switches, a good way to paint neatly around them is to loosen the face plate slightly so that you can paint behind them, before re-attaching them once the paint has dried.

𝒱 Paint a border around the edges using a medium paintbrush. This is called 'cutting in' and, if the walls are a different colour from the ceilings, this is an important part of the process. Other areas you may want to think about 'cutting in' are by window and door frames, any picture and dado rails, and skirting boards. You can use a small or larger brush, whatever you like to use best, but you will need to do it carefully and hold your brush exactly (like a pen) because this will help you keep the line straight. You may also want to pour some paint into a smaller container, so you're not dipping your brush into the massive pot and lugging it around the room with you. Make sure you don't overload your brush; wiggle it into the corners because this will help your brush release more paint. I always have a cloth to wipe away any areas that are not quite right.

𝒱 Start painting the larger areas – just go for it. I get my roller and do my best to cover the larger areas up to the 'cutting in' lines I've just made, and work the paint in around the corners and other tricky areas. It's simpler than you think. I start by placing the roller three quarters of the way up the wall, roll towards the ceiling and then all the way down towards the floor. It's a good idea when working with a large roller to paint in zigzag strokes in different directions, so you get an even coverage, but then finish with strokes all in one direction. I always try to finish one wall at a time without taking a break, so there are no visible lines, streaks or variations in the colour.

𝒱 If you splodge paint down the wall, just notice where it is and work it in with the roller or the brush.

𝒱 Don't ever be guided by the first coat because it's very disheartening. You'll look at the first coat and go, 'Why I am bothering? This looks rubbish!' Trust me – just give it another coat! Deeper colours may even need further coats, but they will completely change the whole appearance of the room. Then you will realise that painting is not as difficult as it looks.

PAINTING CIRCLES

We have a decorative plaster rose on the wall; this is a moulded plaque full of cherubs, and it's so pretty. These kinds of decorative roses are mostly found on ceilings in Georgian and Victorian properties, where a light fitting hangs through the middle, so I wasn't sure what it was doing on my wall, but I definitely didn't want to take it out. I love it. When we moved in it was a sad beige colour. I wanted to make something of it, so I painted it white.

The one thing I would say about painting something round is that it will never, ever look 100 per cent perfect – my painted rose looks a little bit dodgy, but that doesn't bother me. You can't tape that accurately round a curve! If you wanted to, you could make a border with beads or something similar, so if the brush slips, the paint doesn't go on the surrounding wall. I still love my rose though.

LOOK AFTER YOUR PAINTING TOOLS

Look after your tools, they will look after you! It's important to care for things properly, because painting is something you will do regularly in any home. I know washing out paint is a bit of a boring job, but there is nothing worse than a crusty roller! If you are going back to paint the next day, you can swerve the daily clean up by wrapping your brush or roller in plastic, so they don't dry out too much. We were using white paint every day, so we just wrapped those brushes and rollers in clingfilm between each use. I always use a paint tray, so I am not dipping bits of dust stuck on my paintbrush into the tin.

♥ Even if you haven't finished with a tin of paint, always seal the lid completely when not in use. Wipe the lid and lip around the outside of the tin to make sure they are free from drips so it closes fully.

♥ When you've finished with your brush or roller, squeeze out as much paint as you can and then clean it according to the type of paint you've been using. Oil-based paints require more work, and you need to use a solvent like white spirit to get them clean. Once they're clean, dry the brushes and roller with a cloth and leave them to dry out completely.

♥ For paint trays, pour any unused paint back into the tin and rinse under cold water, using a brush to rub off all the excess paint. Use a rag and solvent to remove oil-based paint; for water-based paint, you can let it dry and then peel off the old paint. Before storing, make sure it is completely clean as you don't want to mix yourself a brand-new colour when painting!

USE WHAT YOU ALREADY HAVE

I had some cladding left over from the Blue Loo and I thought, 'Right, I'm going to use that to make myself a little corner.' There are only two small walls in the conservatory, so it felt great to make a bit of a feature with one of them. I did exactly what I did with the loo and went round with the cladding, sticking it with No More Nails. I didn't have any left-over dado rail from the loo but I did have some thin skirting from the boys' room, so I used that as a dado. Then I put up a floating shelf that I decorated with some ornaments. With my special chair and some stools in the corner, I can sit in here with my Marmite on toast in one hand and a Diet Coke in the other (I know, wild!) and just enjoy the room.

Making a Floral Ceiling

Hero task

When we moved in, there was this weird panelled ceiling in the conservatory. I think it might have been a sunscreen as it gets really hot in there during the summer. I didn't like it because it completely blocked out the light. It was hanging on metal rods so I got some pliers and unscrewed the panels and removed them. I was left with two bars across the ceiling. I thought I might take them off and then I thought again. I wondered if I could hang something up there, like flowers?

My first attempt at a floral ceiling didn't look quite right: it looked tacky. I just hung some fejkas over one of the central bars (Joe said it was like walking through a jungle!) I tried to do it the easiest way that I could and I hated it. It didn't bring the room to life in the way I thought it was going to and I knew I had to work a bit harder at it and come up with something different.

I still knew that I wanted flowers up there. So I started looking at flower displays online and I saw that people were using wooden boards to drape their flower displays over. It automatically made it look classier. I wondered what I could do and how I could recreate that look.

A carpenter was doing some work in that room (more on that later!) and I asked him if he had any scrap pieces of wood that were light enough for me to hang from the ceiling. So the next day he brought this big piece of wood over. If you are looking for random items, like pieces of wood, you could go to the tip or look in skips (but always ask before you take anything from a skip or the tip!) or go to the local wood merchants – or ask your carpenter. It only cost me a tenner. He couldn't use the piece or do anything with it, it was just lying around in his workshop.

Never be afraid to ask!

- **I bought some hanging spider lights from Amazon** – this is a light fitting with multiple pendants hanging from a single fixture. Once I had my wood, I drilled large holes through the wood in a zigzag shape along the board – I didn't think too hard about making the spaces between them exact – then I threaded in the two sets of hanging spider lights.

- **I used my staple gun to fix the fake flowers** that I had bought (also from Amazon) in place and draped them over the sides. They were called artificial wisteria vine garland plants and I chose the purple and white ones. I added some eucalyptus that was in a pot from IKEA and laid that across to add some greenery.

- **With the help of my dad**, I hung the board up along the ceiling using all the fixings that were in place from the previous ceiling hangings. An electrician connected the lights to the light fittings for me. It took him about an hour, so I just paid for his time.

KEEP TRYING

I make mistakes all the time and my first flower ceiling was an example of that. It really bugged me, so I had another go. Ask yourself why you don't like it. For me, it was because I could see all the stems of the plants, so it looked messy. I knew I needed something to cover the stems, so I could only see the flowers, and that's how I came up with the idea of the piece of wood. If you don't like something, just keep trying with it and don't give up. You can do it!

Little things I love ♡

STAPLE GUN

I love my trusty staple gun. There's no need for screws and nails, hot glue, or anything else. Using it always feels like I'm getting maximum gains for minimal input. When I was doing the flower wall in Rose's nursery (see page 180), I stapled the flower panels straight to the wall and the staples didn't even show. I think it is one of the easiest tools to use. Even if I am putting fabric around a chair or a piece of wood, I will staple it in place underneath. There's no drying time either. Bonus!

Flower Wall Decorations

I wanted to incorporate more lavender into the decor and also tie in the flower theme from the middle of the room. Looking online I saw loads of displays in test tube-style pots that are glue-gunned directly to the walls and decided to create my own, below the rose wall plaque. It brought me so much joy! It is far from perfect, but I love it.

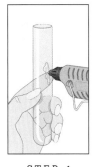
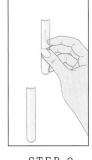

STEP 1   STEP 2   STEP 3   STEP 4

❦ **GATHER YOUR FLOWERS**. I used fejka lavender and plastic test tubes that I bought in bulk from Amazon. They worked out at 50 pence each. I have loads left and I'm sure I'll be able to put them to good use!

❦ **GRAB YOUR GLUE GUN**. Run a thin line of glue down the tube. Press it against the wall and hold in place for a minute or until secure.

❦ **POP FLOWERS IN THE TUBE**, once the glue has dried. So cute! Maybe when Rex is older, he can fill them with real flowers!

❦ **FIX MORE TUBES TO THE WALL**, arranging them randomly or however they look best to you.

Little things I love ♡

FAKE FLOWERS (FEJKAS)

Everyone knows I love my fake potted plants – fejkas – that I buy from IKEA, but I am also mad for fake flowers. I always buy these online from Amazon or eBay. There are some wholesalers but you would have to buy them in bulk to make them cheaper. Unless you are building a whole flower wall, then it's not worth it. My fake flowers and plants make me so happy!

Upcycled Coffee Table

The first time I worked on this coffee table was when Rex went for a nap one day. It was a simple, foldable coffee table from IKEA, although the method I used could work with any coffee table that has a top with lips like a tray. I painted the inside of the tray purple with some paint that I had left over after painting the conservatory walls, stuck down some pebbles in the tray area, and glued some lavender up the legs with my handy glue gun. When it had all dried I realised that the flowers got on my nerves and removed them; helpfully the glue-gun glue just peels off. Resin can be used in loads of crafting projects and makes things so shiny and unique – you can add colour, glitter or in fact anything to it. I wouldn't have added the flowers if I'd known they would annoy me; other than that, this is what I would do:

♡ **PAINT THE INSIDE** of the tray table with any leftover paint. As well as not costing a penny, this is perfect for hiding old drink stains and mug marks.

♡ **PAINT OVER THE SCREWS** in the legs, so they are white or match the rest of the table, so you can't see them.

♡ **MAKE A BORDER** of beads or pebbles inside the tray and glue them down.

♡ **POUR RESIN ON TOP** to fix the beads or pebbles in place and make the surface flat. I knew if I just glued them they would break off, so resin did the job. Resin can be one of those scary materials but you literally just mix it and pour it in – it is made of two parts that when added together harden into a solid glossy plastic. Important note: always do any DIY or crafting with resin in a well-ventilated space, using a mask. Some resins are odourless but that doesn't mean they're not releasing any fumes, so always read the instructions first!

Expert Help ♡

FITTED FURNITURE & FLOORING

Our conservatory is a living space for all of us, but because this room is off the lounge, it made sense to use it for some of the kids' stuff so it doesn't spill into the sitting room. I found a small-business carpenter, who is brilliant and reasonably priced, to make fitted storage all around the room, which gave it a period-home vibe. I love that particular look of some houses and furniture. Because ours isn't a period home, I knew the conservatory was the only room I could create that kind of effect in, because the windows are so tall, so I could carry it off.

I always try and use local businesses where I can. When Rex was born I bought this clothing stand for his clothes from a little local company that makes wooden stands and I got to know them. The brother of the company's owner helps her make them, and he is so clever and underrated. I wanted to give my money to a small business and a local carpenter, so I asked him to do the work.

Each section opens up and the kids' toys are in there; I have labelled all the separate spaces, so the kids know what goes in each box and they are pretty good about putting their stuff away. I am also getting fitted seat cushions, so it can be a sitting area. My top piece of advice: make the lids soft-close, which means using a type of hinge that closes slowly, otherwise the furniture will be ruined, you will have a constant headache with the banging, and who knows how any small hands will fare!

The same guy who did our bathroom, put our flooring into the conservatory. We used a laminate, which is slightly more expensive than vinyl but, because it was a bigger space, the likelihood of vinyl getting ripped up by the boys running around was high, so I knew we needed something a bit more solid and hard-wearing. I think wood is the most beautiful thing in the world and, when all our kids have left home, solid oak floors are the dream, but while they are all here and running around, it's not for us. The laminate was the cheaper alternative to wood, and it was laid on top of the tiles that were already here.

Quick fix

APPLYING CAULK

This is my biggest hero product – caulk is life. If you think something looks a bit shit because it is a little wonky or there are gaps, caulk is the answer. It's really cheap and easy to use and you can put it around skirting boards, window and door frames, or coving; wherever things need a bit of a tidy up. Caulk is a flexible acrylic filler that just makes everything look more finished. Most decorators apply caulk to stuff because it gives everything a neater finish. There was a big gap between the cladding and the skirting and so I ran a line of caulk along the whole thing and now you can't even see it. It changes the whole look of a room. If the gap is really wide, you can use an expanding foam filler but caulk worked for me!

♥ Make sure the area you plan to caulk is clean and free from dust. Just run a damp microfibre cloth over everything.

♥ If you're applying a line of caulk to an area and are worried about getting it straight, you can tape the area first – I just tend to free-style.

♥ I use a normal applicator gun when applying caulk. These are easy to use and with a little bit of practice you will get the hang of it, no problem.

♥ Lay the line of caulk where you want it, squeezing the applicator gun and filling the gap as you go. Keep the motion smooth and swift for an even application. I find I get a better finish when I don't go too slowly. Work at a slight angle to the gap or crack you want to fill. And don't put too much caulk in because you can always add more later.

♥ If you have put masking tape in place, remove it immediately after caulking.

♥ Either wet your finger and run it over the caulk to make it smooth or use a damp sponge. If you're a bit nervous to use your finger, you can get proper angled tools to neaten up the line of caulk. When caulk is still wet, it can be easily removed, so if you make a mistake, just wipe it off and start again.

♥ Once you're happy, leave it and that's it! Thinner layers will always dry a bit more quickly but I tend to leave it for 24 hours before doing anything else.

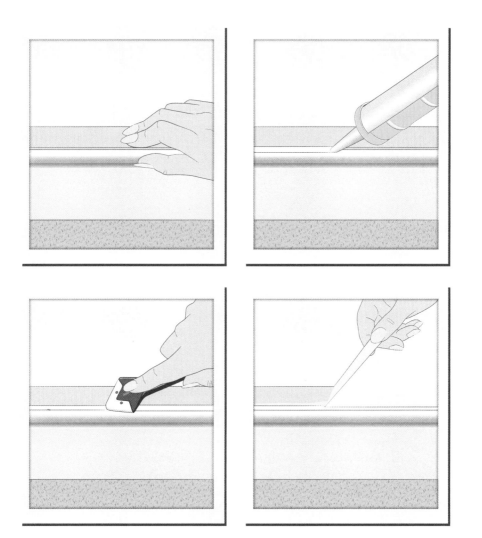

How to

CHOOSE THE RIGHT FILLER

If you have ever been to the caulk aisle at your local DIY store, you will know how much choice there is. Having said that, I don't think it matters too much what type of caulk you use. General decorator's caulk can be used in so many different areas, like filling in the gaps and cracks around window frames, doors, and skirting boards. It's really easy to apply with a applicator gun and dries quickly.

Both caulks and sealants are used to fill gaps and cracks, but silicone sealant is different. This is really elastic and should be used on tiles and for sealing the areas around sinks, showers, and baths, because it's waterproof and better for areas where there is more moisture. It's also more rubbery, so won't tear in larger joints.

I would never put decorator's caulk around a sink but I do sometimes use silicone sealant where I shouldn't. I just experiment loads to see what works best for me. Once dried, caulk is much harder than silicone sealant; sealant is more flexible. There are different colours available for both products, including the standard white, which I use most often.

CRAFTING
Checklist

☐ Scissors

☐ Utility knife

☐ Fejkas *(not a tool, I know, but essential parts of most of my crafting jobs!)*

☐ Glue gun

☐ Tape

☐ String or twine

☐ Pencil

The Bathroom

♡

Inspiration for this bathroom struck me when sitting on the toilet one day.

I was looking around the family bathroom thinking it would be one of the last rooms that we would decorate after our new baby arrived because it was the least important. But then I figured it wouldn't take much work at all to really change how it looked to something pretty glam!

When we did this makeover, we always knew that it was temporary and eventually we would completely re-do this bathroom (I mean, I LOVE a walk-in shower) but I wanted to jazz up what was already there in the meantime. When I first came into this room, I didn't know where to get started and that was part of the reason I didn't think we would crack on with it so quickly. But then I decided to look at the wall with the sink unit and huge cabinet. As much as the sink cabinet was a quality piece of furniture, all the tile grouting was going yellow. But I knew we could just paint the woodwork and tidy up the grout and it would look completely different. There was an awful cabinet in the middle of the wall – we didn't like it at all, and it was completely mirrored so there was no way to change it, so we took it down and recycled it. We swapped it for a flat mirror with a simple black frame to cover the gaps and it does the job perfectly.

Black goes over everything and, with so much dark wood, I knew that if I wanted any other colour, I would need to do a lot of sanding, which can be a bit of a nightmare. Some of the wood is quite old and porous, and once you start sanding this type of wood, it can chip away, so then you worry you are doing it wrong and making it worse. I decided to stick with black paint and only clean the surfaces before painting, rather than doing a big sanding job. I was quite pregnant with Princess Pickle at that stage, so wanted to make do and mend as best I could. We painted all the woodwork (skirting, window frames, sink unit) and then the floor. I added in a load of black accessories, including a black toilet seat and loo brush, toilet roll holder, and black towels and dressing gowns. My kids loved their dressing gowns and said they looked like ninjas in them!

The monochrome black-and-white look felt really fresh and minimalist. I found that by going with this colour theme, and then adding a couple of fake potted succulents into the mix, it suddenly felt like I was at a boutique hotel!

CLEANING AND RE-SEALING TILES

Cleaning up old tiles can really make a bathroom feel so much fresher. The grouting on the tiles in the bathroom was really yellow but rather than replace the tiling, I decided to use elbow grease to spruce the wall up. Taking grout off is a massive job and one I didn't fancy. You can also paint ceramic bathroom tiles with a water-resistant tile paint but I decided just to clean these up.

Grout can become really discoloured with mould and mildew. Yuck! I started trying to clean the tiles and grouting first with a super-scrubber, which is like an electric toothbrush but bigger. There are loads of cleaning products you can use, like bicarbonate of soda and vinegar or even whitening toothpaste, to try to make it whiter. All you need to do is put some cleaning agent on the scrubber (or on the grouted areas) and give it a good wipe or scrub. For me, this grouting was just so disgusting, I realised it was one war that I was never going to win, so I gave up!

You can remove the old grout first using a specialist grout removal blade. If you do this, make sure you protect your eyes and hands. Here, I decided to just re-seal the tiles, and go over the grout with silicone sealer to brighten it up and give the tiles their own personal facelift!

◊ Once you're ready, wipe over the tiles with a damp cloth to remove dust and leave to dry.

◊ I didn't remove the old grout and just went over the top of the existing grout with a silicone sealant. If you want to clean up grout, there are also grout pens, designed just for this job.

◊ I decided to re-seal the tiles. Instead of using my large gun, which I use for applying caulk (see page 114),

I used a small sealant applicator from Unibond called Re-New, which I felt could do the job much more easily. Make sure you look at any instructions before you start.

◊ Make a hole in the nozzle of the applicator and start applying it.

◊ I dragged the silicone sealer into the space in between the tiles. I tried to keep my hand steady and apply constant pressure. If you are a beginner, you may want to use masking tape so you can be sure that your lines are straight. I find that wiping it with a finger is easier than a sponge, but do what works for you.

🤍 If you are doing a bigger area, the bigger tubes cost less than two small ones but are also less easy to use, so once the small tube is finished, re-fill the smaller applicator, so you save money.

🤍 Once you are happy, leave the sealant to dry. If you have added masking tape, be sure to take this off.

🤍 Wait for 24 hours and the job is done! There literally is no better feeling!

Anywhere where there is water and the surround is old, you will need to re-seal: so, around a shower, sink, or bath are all areas that will need to be sealed.

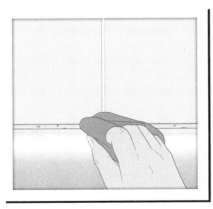

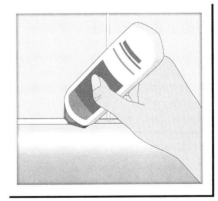

How to

USE COMMAND STRIPS

There load of prints out there that make you giggle. I bought my 'Nakey, nakey, naked' and 'Nice bum' prints from a small business called Mutha Maker. They make me smile! I stuck them up above the loo using Command Strips, another hero product. I use these strips to hang pictures all over the house.

If you have a light picture frame, always use Command Strips. If you are hanging a mirror, don't! People say you can use them for heavier objects but I wouldn't dare. If they fall, you might feel like you are being robbed in the middle of the night! You can use a spirit level for pictures to make sure they are level but I don't always bother.

I love these strips because there's no need to make a hole in the wall, so they're perfect when renting or hanging up anything just for a short time, like Christmas decorations. Unlike Blu Tack that leaves an oily mark and sticky tape that takes paint off, the strips come off cleanly. There are hooks from this brand that can be used in the same way.

❤ Wipe the walls down if they are dirty. If you have just painted a wall, you'll have to wait a week to use the strips.

❤ Rub the wall with some rubbing alcohol. Sometimes I skip this bit, but apparently, it makes the strips stick more.

❤ If your frame has any hooks or other hardware, remove these so the frame will sit flat against the wall. My pictures were just in basic frames.

❤ Separate the strips by tearing them apart and then click two together, pressing them in.

❦ Peel off the liners from one side of the joined strips and stick them onto the back of the frame – I use two at the top and two towards the bottom.

❦ Remove the remaining liners and hold the frame up to the wall, checking that the picture is straight. Push down on the frame to transfer the strips onto the wall. Take the frame away, separating the joined strips as you do so.

❦ Wait 1 hour for the strips to stick fully to the wall before adding the picture frame.

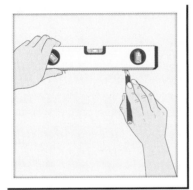

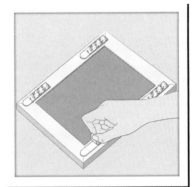

Quick fix

PAINTING FLOOR TILES

Flooring can be tricky but painting is such a cost-effective way of making any floor look SO much better. After we painted the cabinet under the sink black and the surrounding woodwork, both Joe and I thought, 'Why not paint the floor tiles?' We had seen loads of people do it online, so Joe painted these because I was pregnant and was worried about breathing in too many paint fumes. Joe is not a painter but he slapped it on. It was so easy to do and made the bathroom feel huge. We loved the results of this super-chic paint job!

♥ Choose your paint. You can't use any old paint on bathroom tiles – it does need to be specialist floor tile paint.

♥ Clear the floor of any bathroom accessories so that you have a clear run at it. Clean the floor tiles first, making sure they are completely grease-free and dust-free, and leave them to dry. You may want to lightly sand the tiles – ours had quite a rough surface, so the paint went on easily.

♥ Open the doors and windows – the fumes from floor tile paint can be really strong.

♥ Apply a primer first, if you wish (we skipped this bit!). You can prime the tiles using the floor tile paint that you are going to use for the top coats. Just thin it down slightly with one part white spirit to ten parts floor tile paint.

♥ Paint the floor in the same way as you would paint a wall (see page 100), by cutting in along the edges of the floor with a brush and then filling the main area in with a roller. Never pour the paint onto the floor and move it around from there as this will give an uneven finish.

♥ Start painting at the corner furthest from the door. Don't paint yourself into the room as Joe did. He left sock marks everywhere – I have no idea how he ninja'd himself out of there!

♥ Let the first coat dry for a day or two before applying another coat. Remember the bathroom will be out of action, so if it's your only one, sweet-talk your neighbours!

♥ Once dry, apply a sealant. It was easy to see when our tiles were dry because they went from shiny to matt. Apply two or three coats of sealant, letting each one dry first.

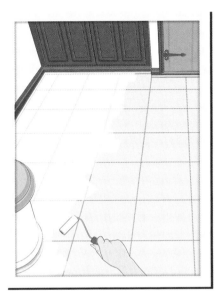

PAINTING IN BLACK AND WHITE

What I would say about painting black skirting and white walls? I'd
say that I should have sealed the frog tape in first before painting
the skirting boards to get a completely straight line. I should have
painted the white first (always paint the lighter colour first) and
once it was completely dry, after two or three days, I should have
frog-taped that line using a spirit level so it was completely straight.
I should have then sealed it with a clear lacquer and left it to dry
completely and then painted the skirting. The lacquer would've
acted as a barrier to stop the paints bleeding or smudging into
each other. I didn't do this – I drove myself to distraction painting
black, then white, then black, then white to try to make the line
straight. I'm not sure why I did it to myself! So silly!

How to

PAINT A WINDOW FRAME

I know painting window frames might seem a bit more intimidating than simply whacking the roller around on walls and ceilings, but it is really satisfying. It can also completely transform the look of your windows. There are special paints for certain materials, and there is even a specific type of paint for uPVC windows, if you want to do more than just clean them up.

- Choose your paint colour. Light colours can have a brightening effect or you can make a statement with a bolder shade. The window frames can also be the same colour as your walls – there are no rules when choosing paints. I chose black because the woodwork was so dark.

- Sand the frames down first using sandpaper. (Don't forget to wear your goggles!)

- Clean the frame by wiping away any dust with a damp cloth and leave to dry.

- For neat painted edges, run masking tape around the window panes. Don't remove the masking tape until you've finished and the paint is completely dry, otherwise you will end up taking loads of the paint with it and have to start again. Sometimes I skip the masking tape stage and just have a damp cloth to hand to wipe any areas that are not quite perfect.

- If you are extra-worried about paint splashes, you can tape over newspaper to cover the panes completely.

- Never overload your brush with too much paint as this may cause drips or the paint to pool in the corners of the frame. For better coverage, you can always go over the paintwork a few times.

- Paint in a consistent direction with short, even brush strokes.

- Start from the top and paint downwards, finishing with the window-sill and outer frames.

- Check for any drips or pooling paint, then leave the frame to dry completely before adding another coat, if you want. You might like to open the window to help everything dry more quickly. It is a good idea to start this job earlier in the day, so you can leave the windows open for the rest of the day to let the paint dry.

- Stand back and admire your work!

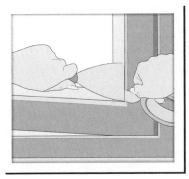

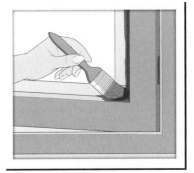

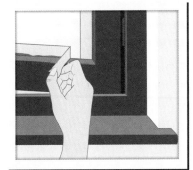

Quick fix

ADD A BATHROOM LIGHT PULL CHAIN

I think a pull chain or string for a bathroom light is much better for kids because they can reach it. In most bathrooms there are pull-cord switches mounted to the ceiling so you can switch the light on and off with wet hands and not be electrocuted. There are loads of different designs that you can source online. Ours is a lovely one with a ceramic pull and light chain. I think the chain is much nicer than a piece of string and feels a bit more special.

SKIP THE BLACK LOO ROLL

The black accessories like the loo brush, towels, and loo seat were great. But the black loo roll was so unfortunate. There's a reason why most loo paper is pale-coloured. I was never sure what was going on there or whether I had done well with it! I just had to wipe and hope for the best.

How to

CHANGE A TOILET SEAT

Did you know you can change a loo seat in just a few minutes? I know, right, who knew?! Whether your old one is looking tired or you want a new colour, changing a loo seat can easily update the look of the room. I chose a new black one for our bathroom. I also changed the one in the Blue Loo from brown to white 'cos it made me feel a bit gross as it looked like there was wee in the toilet the whole time from the reflection of the brown seat!

♥ There are different shapes of toilet bowl. Most are round or oval, but some are D-shaped or square. Seats are adjustable to fit the most common bowl shapes. Measure up to double-check the size you need.

♥ The measurements you need are: the distance between the seat-fixing screw holes, the width of the bowl at its widest, and the length from the front of the bowl back to where the two screw holes are.

♥ Remove the old seat by taking off the fittings using a screwdriver to lift any caps and remove any screws. You may need pliers to remove any nuts.

♥ Use the hinges to move the new seat into place to fit the holes in the bowl. Follow the instructions to adjust the position. Secure them using any screws provided (or your own).

♥ Sit the long bolts into place. Don't drop anything in the loo while completing this bit!

♥ Move the seat into position. Secure it in place with nuts and bolts. If they includes washers, put these on first, under the nuts. Don't overtighten.

Upcycling Old Bottles

I love a quick and easy crafting project! If you have any pretty bottles that you love and have used up the contents inside, rather than throwing them away and buying new ones, reuse them. Sometimes I will turn an old perfume bottle into a reed diffuser, or stick a candle in it, but in my bathroom I have a few bottles I use for my favourite bathroom products.

Simply soak the label and peel it off; if there's a sticky residue, run water over the bottle and give it a clean (put it through the dishwasher if you like!). When it's completely dry, put your own label on. I have glass bottles that I put my own stickers on and it makes them completely your own. I then fill them up with my favourite products, whether it is hand soap or bath salts.

BREAK UP MONOCHROME

I love the monochrome look in this bathroom but you need to break it up a bit with greenery to give it more character and texture. Black and white on its own can feel a bit austere and clinical. Whenever I look at plants it makes me think of life, so they make a room feel alive. I know I have a fake plant problem, but I think these succulents and other fejkas always look a bit tropical and like I might be on holiday somewhere!

I always add the odd soft furnishing to soften the place up too. I bought a new black and cream rattan rug from Dunelm to put under the sink – it was just £3. Bargain!

How to

CHANGE A LIGHTBULB

It is easy to get confused with different types of lights and I think some people think spotlights are not easy to change. With downlights, they are just in the ceiling rather than below the ceiling!

Here is my guide:

- First of all, make sure the power is switched off. The safest way to do this is to switch it off at the fusebox. There should be a big red 'off' button.

- Let it cool, so the bulb is never hot or warm to touch.

- If you are changing the lightbulb in a ceiling light, use a step ladder so you can safely reach it.

- For bayonet lightbulbs (the twist and lock type) push upwards and twist anti-clockwise to remove. They can be quite delicate, so don't squeeze too hard. For screw-fitting blubs, simply unscrew by turning the bulb anti-clockwise. With downlights, look for the metal ring and squeeze the brackets together and remove the old lightbulb.

- Put in the replacement bulb lightly but firmly into the socket by either turning it clockwise until it clicks into place or by screwing it in clockwise. For downlights, fit the new bulb by aligning the pins and clicking back into place.

- Once the bulb is in, turn the power back on and switch on the light.

- Dispose of the bulb, well out of the reach of any small hands.

ALWAYS CHOOSE LED LIGHTS

When we moved into Pickle Cottage, all our light fittings had traditional bulbs. Our electricity bill the first month was extortionate – I almost fainted when I saw it.

LED lights use a lot less energy (so they are much better for the environment) and can sometimes pay for themselves in a couple of months. Although the upfront cost might be a bit more, you will definitely see savings in the long-term. They will get bright the minute that you turn them on and they are ultra-long-lasting. The quality of the different bulbs can vary, so make sure you opt for a reliable and trusted brand. After that first month, we went around the house and changed every single bulb to an LED one. Replacing normal bulbs with LED ones is fairly simple. Most of them are compatible with normal fixtures.

Each one has a different 'temperature' measured in Kelvin. I like warmer white lights that are about 2700 Kelvin.

Little things I love ♡

LADDER SHELF

When it came to accessorising the bathroom, there were floating shelves that I had bought for the downstairs loo; they were not the right colour, but I kept them because I knew I would use them somewhere else, so I used them in here. I also had an old ladder shelf that was in Harry's (Joe's eldest's) bedroom and he didn't want it anymore because it was too bulky.

When I originally bought it, Joe went mad. He was like: 'Ladder shelf. What the hell is a ladder shelf?' 'It's a shelf that looks like a ladder,' I told him!

I love this type of shelving because you can display accessories really easily, and they are more affordable than some other types of large shelving units – this one was only £25. I put some fake plants and candles on this and it really cheered the room up.

MY BATHROOM ACCESSORIES
Checklist

- [ ] Toilet seat
- [ ] Loo roll holder
- [ ] Loo brush
- [ ] Bath mat
- [ ] Storage baskets
- [ ] Mirror
- [ ] Floating shelves
- [ ] Containers with labels
- [ ] Candles
- [ ] Fejkas
- [ ] Prints or wall decor
- [ ] Ladder shelf *(if you have space)*

The Garden

♡

The first time
we drove up the
long driveway to
Pickle Cottage,
the surrounding
countryside took
my breath away.

I couldn't believe how beautiful the garden was – it felt like something out of a fairytale. Even now, every time I arrive home after being at work or out with friends or family, it makes me feel really emotional.

We all fell in love with the garden and the views of the fields all around the cottage. There are so many different and magical parts to it. I knew the kids would spend hours running around the lawns and through the woods. I know it sounds really stupid, but each time I see a new flower appear in the garden, I think to myself 'I can't believe that is OUR flower.' It just makes me want to cry.

When I first walked out there, the garden felt vast. There is a Wendy house that I have done up for Rex, a greenhouse where we've grown tomatoes and other veggies, and an old swimming pool that we have been slowly revamping. I will talk you through each of these projects in this chapter. If you're working on creating a beautiful space indoors, always think about the outdoors too. Even if it's just a small patio, you can jet wash it and try to grow plants in pots on there. During the renovations, while the house has been hectic, I've found our garden such a sanctuary. When there is dust and mess everywhere, I make a cup of tea and sit in my egg chair or on one of the benches and take a few breaths.

The day we put up the garden swing felt so special. As a kid that would've been my absolute dream. I'll never forget the boys' faces when they saw it. One day, we also discovered another swing under the arches. There was a metal chain wrapped around one of the arches. We were all like, 'What is that?' and when we unwrapped it, it was like a bonus swing. It was like something out of the Secret Garden!

Along one side of our garden, I've installed these cute solar lights that look like mini dancing flames. All you need to do is set them up and let the energy from the sun do its work During the summer evenings, the boys play outside in the light from these. I love it when it's dark outside and these solar lights give the garden a really special warm glow.

Quick fix

JET WASHING

Jet washing – also called pressure washing – has to be the ultimate quick fix.
I bloomin' love it. It is right up there with caulking. I jet-washed everything
possible in our garden; there were two benches outside, the roof of the Wendy
house, the large paving stones on the ground, pots, the gate, and the patio.
I invested in a really good jet washer. I think I might actually be addicted to jet
washing! I mean I even pressure washed my oven trays and Rex's highchair –
not sure if that is recommended but it got them clean in about five seconds!

♥ Take off anything attached to
whatever it is you are jet washing,
so nothing flies off.

♥ Connect the hose to the jet washer
and the tap, then make sure water
is running through it. Connect to the
mains electricity supply.

♥ Don't get too close to whatever you
are jet washing. The pressure of the
jet can be pretty powerful so, if it's
something like limestone or wood,
you run the risk of chipping or
damaging it if you get too near.

♥ Most jet washers have three
settings. Don't do what I do – go in
on the highest and most powerful
one. It strips everything! Familiarise
yourself with the different settings

and what materials they are for
before you start, because there are
different strengths and shapes of jet
spray. Decking and wooden objects
will need a different setting from
tougher materials, so if you were
jet washing your driveway, say, you
would need more power.

♥ Point and go! So, so satisfying!

♥ You can add a special detergent for
stubborn stains, but I find that water
on its own normally does the job.

♥ If you have cleaned wooden
furniture, let it dry completely and
then stain and seal it. This will make
your furniture look smart and help
to protect it from the elements. Let
the stain dry for at least 24 hours.

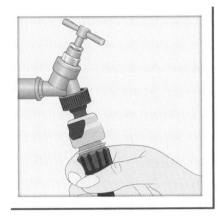

Renovating a
Wendy House

The Wendy house was so beautiful. I fell in love with it as soon as I saw it, and so did Rex. However, some of the wood was quite rotten. With wood rot, you can treat it with a wood filler and try to restore it that way, but my dad and I decided to replace all the bad planks with new ones. It was a labour of love.

If you have a similar project, I would say weigh up what you have: it it's a repair job, that's OK (this was a big one and we had to go back almost to square one!) but if the structure is completely rotten, you may need to start again from scratch. We knew that because this was outdoors, we could spend more money repairing the walls than replacing them. So we used special plywood that's for outdoor use to reinforce the walls inside. We then sealed them with a silicon sealant, so the house was completely watertight. Then we got busy painting and sealing the outside – what we did can apply to any type of outdoor furniture.

- ♡ **Once we had the structure in place**, we sanded it down, so the paint and sealant would adhere to the wood. We then applied two coats of exterior acrylic paint to the wood. I used lighter whites and greys to make it look a bit fresher, and knew I could always go over it in a darker colour if that didn't work.

- ♡ **We allowed each coat to dry** before applying the next one.

- ♡ **We then sealed it with two coats of wood sealant**. This stops it from warping, rotting, or cracking. Apply the sealant with a clean brush, putting it on evenly along the grain of the wood. Very porous woods may need more than two coats.

- ♡ **I tried to add a little mini white picket fence** – I'm not going to lie, this wasn't the most successful as the ground was SO hard. The spiked bits should have just slipped into the ground easily and the sections interlinked together. But I almost broke my back pushing!

- ♡ **I added a door mat** – 'Little Pickle Cottage' – and a pretty door hanging with yellow flowers and a vase to make it seem really welcoming. Rex was right in there – I mean who wouldn't be?!

Quick fix

STENCILLING PAVING STONES

The paving stones leading to the Wendy house were all different sizes and, when I jet-washed them, I could see that they were also various colours. I decided to paint over them using floor paint to give them a uniform look. Most exterior paint work on stone should be done using masonry paint but I had this paint that I knew would be quite hard-wearing and be able to withstand the weather. I wasn't sure if it would work but it hasn't come off yet! I love stencilling and I think it can transform an uneven or grubby patio and make it look really special, without having to pull the whole thing up and start again. I think it can also make an outdoor space feel like a living space. Budget makeover goals!

♥ Find the stencil that you want to use. If you Google 'patio stencils' there are loads of designs available. I chose a stencil in a pretty fleur-de-lis pattern made from flexible plastic, so I can use it forever. Make sure the paint you are using is suitable for outdoor use. There are loads of garden paints available. I used white paint over grey paving stones.

♥ Our paving stones were rough sandstone, so I taped the stencil down with frog tape on each slab. You can use a low-tack adhesive spray to keep the stencil in place, which helps to stop the paint bleeding underneath the stencil.

♥ Use a small foam roller to go over the stencil with a light pressure. I used a roller at first but it kept slipping, so I found I had more control with a paintbrush. Don't

overload your roller or brush with paint and use a light pressure, so the paint does not bleed underneath the stencil. Sometimes less is more!

♥ If your stones are uneven like mine, you will have to work the paint into the uneven bits. You can always practise on a piece of paper first.

♥ After you've painted each one, peel the stencil off carefully. Wipe the stencil down if it gets clogged up with excess paint, so it's completely clean before you move on to the next stone. Be careful when laying the stencil down on the new design that you don't smudge the one you've just done.

♥ Take it slowly and be methodical! Depending on the type of paint you've used, once it has dried, you might want to use a sealant.

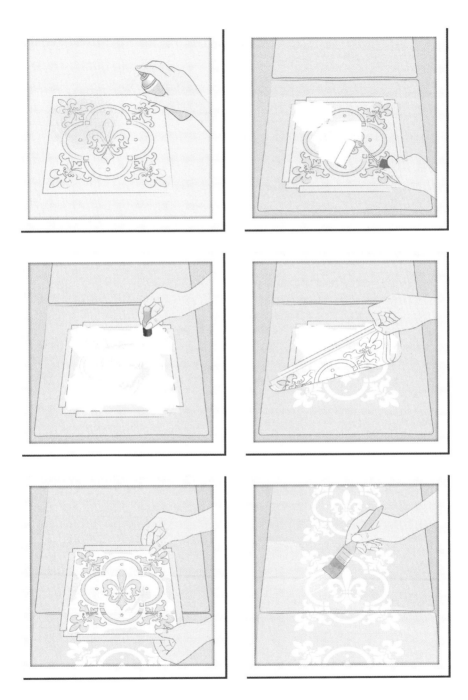

GROW PLANTS IN A GREENHOUSE

I'm all over the greenhouse! My grandad used to have an amazing greenhouse where he grew strawberries, tomatoes, cucumbers, and other fruit and veg. I would sit at the dinner table and he would serve up everything from his garden – it was just the best food you had ever tasted.

When I saw the greenhouse at Pickle Cottage, I knew I had to grow something. To start with, I took on more than I should have done. I ended up growing sweetcorn, peppers, lettuce, and tomatoes and it grew into a jungle in there. Some plants lived, some didn't, and some just hung on! The tomatoes did well, growing at a rate of knots, so I would say: start with them as they will grow anywhere.

Growing your own is a commitment. You need the time to look after the plants in your greenhouse. Out of everything, tomatoes are probably the least amount of work; they need watering and a quick prune from time to time but are easier than some other things. Take carrots, for example: you can start them in the greenhouse but you will need to keep a good eye on them because, eventually, they will need to be re-potted and then planted outside. It's a full-time job!

In the situation we are now with kids and work, we need easy stuff to grow, because looking after a plant is like having another child! Rex and I try to go into the greenhouse every morning and night to give them a drink. We use rainwater from butts that we have outside our greenhouse, which collect water from the gutters. The tap to the butt is really low down, so Rex can fill up his watering can.

Here are my helpful tomato growing tips:

◊ When you're starting out, try growing a few different varieties of tomato – some may like it at your place more than others.

◊ Choose blight-resistant varieties, especially if you're growing your tomatoes outside. Tomato blight is a plant disease that can kill tomatoes in less than a week (yikes!). Tomatoes grown in greenhouses are less likely to be affected.

◊ If you're growing what are called cordon tomatoes – ones that have a long stem and need to grow up a support – pinch out the side-shoots, or clip them off, like a tomato haircut, so the plants put more energy in growing fruit on the main stem.

◊ Tomatoes love lots of sun. If you don't have a greenhouse in your garden, you can put them in a sunny spot on a balcony or by a window.

◊ Little and often is best when it comes to watering tomato plants as it encourages steady growth.

◊ Water the soil, not the plant – tomato plants really hate getting their leaves wet.

◊ Give your plants some liquid tomato food – they'll love it.

◊ You can also mix some concentrated garlic in with your water, which kills pests.

◊ With plenty of sunshine, the green fruits will turn into red tomatoes – so don't panic!

Little things I love ♡

GARDEN SWING

As a little girl, I would have done anything to have a swing in my garden. To fulfill that childhood dream, I decided to install a rope swing on one of my favourite trees in the Pickle Cottage garden, a beautiful willow. I bought the swing, with a solid oak seat and natural ropes to hang it with, from Fall With Grace. We had the wooden swing seat carved with a special message for our boys, which we're now changing now to include Rose too.

Little things I love ♡

MY EGG CHAIR

When Rex was born, I really struggled and whenever
he was unsettled I would sit with him in the egg chair
and he would always calm down. Even now, whenever
he is aggy I take him there; I mean, which baby
doesn't love being hugged and swung?

I have such an emotional attachment to that chair.
For his first birthday, I decorated it with fake flowers
and vines and hung it in the lounge. It was far
too bulky to have in there, so I had to take it back
outside. Now it is under the willow tree by the swing,
so I can watch the boys playing on the swing and sit
there and have a few moments of peace.

How to

ORGANISE YOUR GARDEN BITS 'N' BOBS

My main garden storage is my junk trunk, which is basically storage for all the things I don't want in the house but can't bear to throw away. It's stuff that should probably be in the bin or recycled, like old glass jars and bottles that I think I might be able to use one day in my crafting. Old wrapping paper, old boxes, wire hangers... you need something random, it will probably be in there!

Everything I throw away goes in the bins, also in the garden, but my sister and I have made it our mission to make our bin area a bit prettier. I have massive labels on the bins (so the boys can't pretend that they don't know which bin stuff needs to be thrown into!). I plan to either spray paint the bins a camouflage colour or use greenery panels to hide them. The other idea we had was to grow a little secret hedge area to put the bins behind, but that would take a bit longer to grow.

If you have a garden shed, my main advice would be to use shelves to store all your garden bits and bobs. Never throw any old scrap wood away and use it as a shelf instead. In my last house, I even attached a crate to the wall. I put little hooks on the bottom of the crate where I hung my gloves, spade, and other gardening tools.

Coconut Shell Bird Feeder

I bought and made loads of bird feeders so the birds come to our garden. One of my favourite ones is a natural coconut feeder; they are so easy to make and you can give the birdies extra food, especially when they need it, like during the winter months. Dad helps me with my bird food – he knows which birds like which maggots! When he's around, it's some sort of all-you-can-eat bird buffet.

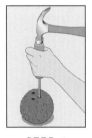

| STEP 1 | STEP 2 | STEP 3 | STEP 4 |

🖊 **MAKE HOLES IN THE COCONUT** using either a hammer and chisel or use your drill. Always drill with your drill pointing towards the ground for safety! Let the coconut water drain out.

🖊 **BREAK THE COCONUT IN HALF** to make two basket shapes. Remove the coconut flesh (or let the birds eat it) to leave just the shell.

🖊 **FILL THE COCONUT SHELL** with shop-bought or homemade suet and add some unsalted seeds (this can be really fun to make yourself and is a fab activity if you have little ones at home).

🖊 **PLACE THE BIRD FEEDER IN A TREE** where cats and squirrels cannot reach it. If you want to hang your coconut shell on a branch, drill holes around the top edge and thread garden string through the holes.

Little things I love ♡

OUTDOOR MIRRORS & RUGS

Mirrors and rugs are not just for indoors, but for outdoors too! Mirrors can make anywhere look amazing and the reflections always create the illusion of more space. They make me feel calm and tranquil.

You don't want the birds to fly into your mirror, so you can buy stickers that make it look like a mirror but are anti-reflective, so they don't smack into them. I also have a cover for my mirror that is waterproof.

You can also buy fantastic outdoor rugs that look really fluffy and soft and feel great but are made from recycled plastics. They are beautiful. I have some under a tree and it is like a little safe haven for me and my babies. Before, the area was a shed and a pile of dirt, but now with a couple of mirrors and a rug and some deckchairs, it feels like a sanctuary.

How to

MAKE YOUR GARDEN PARTY-READY

One of my favourite memories of the garden was my baby shower. It felt like the perfect day and my sister did such an amazing job. She worked so hard and I had no idea it was going to be so special. No matter the size of your garden, I think there are some ways to make it party-ready. You don't even need your own garden – I often see parties being held in parks, too.

♥ Hide the less pretty areas. We are lucky with the views at Pickle Cottage but when she was planning my baby shower my sister said that one of the hardest parts was hiding one corner of the garden that is not so pretty. She managed to do this by putting a tent area there.

♥ Make space for the kids. I think keeping the kids entertained is really important. Happy kids = happy parents. For my baby shower, we had some little tables with craft activities that the kids enjoyed.

♥ Contain it. That really helps the atmosphere, because if your garden is bigger, people tend to spread out and go off in different groups, so having a corner where everyone mingles together is important.

♥ Decorate. There are loads of things you can do yourself to decorate, like putting up bunting, lanterns, or homemade canopies. For my party, my sister did an incredible job using small businesses – she paid for everything – and they dressed the area so it looked amazing.

THE POOL

When we viewed Pickle Cottage, we couldn't believe
there was a swimming pool in the garden. Never in a
million years did I ever imagine owning a house with a
pool. Ordinarily, I would not go for a house with a pool
because they scare the living daylights out of me. If we
didn't have four boys all screaming at us and telling
us to keep it, I would have happily filled it in! First off,
we cleaned it up with the help of a pool man. I spent a
long time staring at him and his specialist equipment
that day. His jet wash was even bigger than ours.
Jet wash goals!

Next, we filled the pool up with water but then quickly
realised that we couldn't easily buy a safety cover for
the pool because it is an unusual kidney shape. So we
drained it immediately. I just couldn't sleep at night
with that pool full of water! I was so paranoid that
someone might fall in – not only the kids, but one of
the dogs, or another animal that might wander into the
garden. It didn't even bear thinking about.

It became clear that our first priority was to work out how to make the pool safe and for me to make peace with it. We considered loads of safety options, like a fence, but I was still worried that animals might get under it or teenagers could get over it. We needed a proper industrial safety cover put over the pool – a retractable cover that is fixed in the ground at one end and that rolls out along on tracks on each side of the pool, completely sealing the water and the surrounding edges of the pool. The cover we chose uses special keys to lock it in place and is super-safe. At the time of writing, the cover is still being made, so I really hope lives up to expectations!

In order for the safety cover to run along the straight tracks, the cover must be rectangular, but our pool was kidney shape. This meant we needed to cut into the ground around the pool to make a rectangular border just outside the kidney-shaped pool. As we would be excavating the soil around the pool, we thought this would be a good opportunity to extend the pool a little at one end to make a shallow splash area, which would be better for Rex and Rose. We also wanted to put in some steps leading down into the pool because they had either been removed at some point or they were never there in the first place!

We needed to find someone to supply and fit our chosen safety cover over the pool. It's not quite like finding an electrician or a plumber as it is a really specialist job. The whole process of hiring someone to do the building work on the pool and supply and fit the safety cover taught me a real lesson. The company we initially found told us they would be able to complete the work quickly. We were promised that the pool would be ready for our first summer at Pickle Cottage, but that didn't happen and it was not even nearly ready by that time. In the end, that company just quit the job. We felt like we had been left in the lurch. We had asked all the right questions, but I think they just realised they had taken on too much. It was really disheartening. Whatever the scale of your project, if you're hiring tradespeople then there are lots of specific questions that you should ask anyone who might be working on your home. I've put all my best advice into the tips for hiring tradespeople, starting on page 162. And should things not go to plan for you (although I really hope they do) then I've given some suggestions for how to put things right on page 164.

Happily, we found a fantastic new firm of pool specialists who have reshaped the pool, installed the new steps and tiled the whole thing with the most beautiful pearlescent grey mosaic tiles. I just love 'em. Rex had a great time hanging out with the guys, who were completely brilliant with him; he totally chewed their ears off with all his questions!

In the area immediatley next to the pool, I have constructed a wooden pergola that I have stained to match the colour of the bark of the surrounding trees. It's going to take a while, but I plan to grow a vine over the pergola so that the leaves will provide some natural shade. And then at the end of the pergola we have built an outdoor fireplace with a chimney out of brick so that we can spend long summer evenings out in the garden.

We're so close to completing the work on the pool area now. It might be a year later than I first thought, but I am excited to take a dip over summer – I know it will be worth the wait!

How to

FIND THE RIGHT TRADESPEOPLE

Finding the right tradesperson or contractor to do a job is never easy. There are sites like Checkatrade and Trustatrader, where people make recommendations, or you can ask friends and family. When it comes to specialist stuff, like major building work or, for us, the swimming pool, I think it's important to learn about whatever it is you need doing. It's vital to educate yourself, so you know the language the tradespeople will be using and can challenge them if they have different ideas from your own. It's good to have some knowledge. One swimming-pool company told me it would take four weeks to complete the project. Even at the time that seemed really far-fetched. If I'd had a better understanding of the work involved, I would have been able to ask them why they were over-promising.

Sometimes what you want done and what they want to do are not the same. Each tradesperson will have jobs they like doing, other work to go to afterwards, stuff that makes them more profit. All contractors will have their own agenda and that's fine because you have yours, too. What you want might not be the best or easiest solution but it's what you want. Yes, they are the experts, but that doesn't mean their way is the only way. Listen to what they say, but don't feel obliged to agree with them. Remember, the big stuff is like the small stuff: you can do whatever you want! It might take longer or be more expensive but it is your home. That's why it is so important to know a bit about what you are talking about. Don't feel pushed into something because someone more qualified has told you how to do it. If, in your head, you feel like your life will be better if something is done in a certain way, fight for it. Say, 'Can you please make that happen.' You don't want to be left with the heartache of spending a fortune and not getting what you wanted in the first place.

MY OTHER TOP TIPS:

✔ Get at least three written quotes that include all the material costs before deciding on who to use. Study the quotes carefully. Sometimes the cheapest option is not the best. I think most of the time you get what you pay for.

✔ Be guided by your friends and family. I always recommend good people that I have used. Ask all the questions: What did they do? Did they turn up on time? How much did it cost? Then go online to find out what previous clients think. Google the company and words 'review', 'complaint', or 'recommend'.

✔ Don't be rushed into making a decision. Ask lots of questions. Can they supply references? Are they on review websites? Are they insured? You should 100 per cent be able to take your time. If a tradesperson doesn't want to spend their time with you talking about what you want, definitely look elsewhere.

✔ Be clear about the finished result you want. Don't let anyone talk you out of it. You are in control. Always ask why they are doing something in a certain way. Never be afraid of being annoying – they are working on your home, after all.

✔ Go small whenever possible! Small firms don't have the same overheads as larger organisations, so they can often do the work more cheaply.

✔ Never pay in full up front. This is the most important rule. If a company you are hiring says they need a deposit for materials, then negotiate that amount and never pay more than 15 per cent. Set a payment schedule and only pay the final amount when you're completely happy with their work.

✔ Ask for fully itemised invoices that give a breakdown of every cost rather than one overall amount. That way you can see exactly where your money is going and that no sneaky extra costs have been added.

✔ Check for a guarantee. Do they offer guarantees on their work or do the products they are installing come with manufacturers' guarantees? This means you'll be protected if they go bust or any faulty items will be replaced for free.

✔ Limited businesses file their accounts at Companies House, so you can find out who the directors are and how long they have operated. If they have a history of setting up and folding companies in quick succession, that is a huge red flag.

WHAT TO DO WHEN YOU ARE RIPPED OFF

Sometimes we have an idyllic view of how things should be, but they may not go to plan. There is always a risk, and people do get stung. There are some incredible tradespeople out there but there are always those who get it wrong. Sometimes it's not about cowboy builders who want your money, it's tradesmen who have taken on too much work or bitten off more than they can chew. Sometimes they are not bad people but they have made bad business decisions. But, sometimes, there are people who are out to get you.

If you feel you have paid too much for what has been done, there are different ways to sort it out. The reality is that it would cost a lot of money to hire lawyers.

❦ **Talk it through**. My first step would be to try to talk about it. Try really hard to not get too angry or upset (even though you might be really devastated). Look at the facts: you have paid for a service or materials or whatever and you do not think that service has been provided. Try to negotiate with them to get to an agreed point where the work they've done is worth the money you have paid. Ask them to not run away and leave you in the lurch. Maybe they can do something additional – say, complete a day's painting or whatever skillset they may have that you would otherwise have to pay someone else for. I really think trying to negotiate is the best first step.

❦ **Check for insurance and protection schemes**. Ideally, it is always best to check if any tradesperson working on your home is part of a trade association before you start working with them. This can give you extra security, and some have insurance or protection schemes, or can help to resolve any problems or disputes.

❦ **No win, no fee**. You can make a claim with a 'no win, no fee' solicitor for all sorts of reasons: incompetent building work, using defective materials, payment disputes, or work that does not follow building specifications are just a few of them. The truth is, if you have been done over, you may well win but sometimes you won't see the money or it will only come back in dribs and drabs. I would always try to avoid that situation altogether.

EMPLOYING
TRADESPEOPLE
Checklist

- [ ] Ask to see their portfolio of work
- [ ] Check their references and ratings
- [ ] Look them up at Companies House
- [ ] Ask if they will be subcontracting any part of the job
- [ ] Compare written quotations
- [ ] Ask whether they guarantee their work and for how long
- [ ] Check their qualifications *(anyone working with gas must be Gas Safe registered)*
- [ ] Find out if they are VAT registered
- [ ] Find out if they are insured
- [ ] Agree a schedule of works
- [ ] Agree a payment schedule

Rose's Nursery

♡

I adored creating my little girl's nursery; I was in fejka heaven! The small room was a completely blank canvas so I needed to get creative.

I wanted to make sure the room had everything our baby and I needed, but don't get me wrong... decorating this room was solely for me! As I worked on each hero project or quick fix, it made me so thrilled to think that she would be with us soon, looking back at me in the mirror, and being here in this room. It gave me butterflies and made me cry.

When you are creating a nursery, it is really important to remember that it doesn't matter too much what you have in there. We panic ourselves to within an inch of our lives about having 'all the right stuff' but this is not so vital. I knew I needed a cot for her to sleep in and somewhere to store her clothes, and we had enough space to do that, but fourth time around, I have really learned that the main thing you need when it comes to raising a new-born is support.

This room was entirely for me. The baby would be none the wiser! It was for my enjoyment, excitement, and to take my mind off somewhere magical while I was doing it. None of it was essential. I wanted to enjoy it and love the process. If your DIY is slowing down and you are struggling to keep the momentum up (let me tell you – some days I just want to lie down in a dark room and not move), try to find a space you can make for yourself. Then you can go as crazy or as subtle as you would like with it, and do what you want. It could be a spare room or even a spot under the stairs, or in a corner of a separate room. I promise it will make you really happy and give you that kick up the backside to keep going, once you have seen what you have created at the end of it. Magic!

THINK ABOUT THE WALLS

When I started on this room, the walls were so uneven and bowed that I knew I would have to tackle them one at a time and just look at each wall as an individual project. Sometimes when I look at the walls in a room, I think they look flat and boring. As far as I am concerned wall space is space to fill! The nursery is tiny so we knew that we wouldn't be able to have much furniture in there or stuff on the floor, so I decided to add character by putting things on the walls, like wooden panelling and other textures.

USE A #HASHTAG

If you are stuck for ideas, Instagram can be a treasure trove. For panelled walls, for example, hashtags like #wallpanelling and #wallpanellingideas can be a great start. As well as styles, you can decide whether you would like to panel half of your room or the whole room. For me, I've found so many really small businesses that I love by using the hashtag #supportsmallwithstace. If you want to find something really unique that no one else has, then the smaller the business, the better.

Wall Panelling

In the Blue Loo, I clad the lower parts of the walls to divide the space up but I wanted to do something a bit more special in Rose's nursery. There were two lights on the wall already that I wanted to keep but at the same time add character and make it all look a bit more modern. It felt like whole-wall panelling was a real trend that I kept seeing everywhere, with grids on walls to give that 3D-look. I knew it would be a great way of disguising the uneven wall and so I decided to go for it! It was a labour of love!

I watched video tutorials that said it would take a day but it took me a number of days to get right. You might think, 'I can't do this because of x, y, or z' but once you've started you have to power through. Panelling is a really good way to disguise wonky walls, so I thought that – done right – it could hide loads of stuff.

Get planning. This is an important part of the process. There are lots of different styles of panelling to choose from, such as tongue and groove cladding (like those I used in the Blue Loo, see page 32) to portrait panels. I planned to use panelling strips, creating frames in a simple and classic grid design, as this room is not big and I didn't want to make it too fussy or overwhelming. The wall was also completely clear, so I didn't have to worry about working around radiators or any other features.

Measure your walls. First of all, I measured the height and width of the walls. While doing this, I could immediately tell that the walls were completely bowed and so I knew I would have my work cut out here. I went to B&Q to get the panelling strips, and while I was there I rang Joe to ask him to double-check the measurements of the wall again. He told me the height of the room was 93cm. This made me lose my shit! I mean Rex was around 90cm tall, so I knew that was wrong. We don't live in a house for elves!

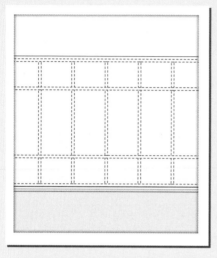

- **Design your panels**. Decide how many frames you would like across your wall and what fits best. I knew I wanted my wall to be divided vertically (from floor to ceiling) into six sections, and horizontally (from corner to corner) into three. This meant six long vertical frames in the middle, bordered by six smaller, squarer frames above and below.

- **Buy the right amount of panelling** based on your measurements. I chose MDF panel strips. You can either cut the strips to length yourself or ask the staff at the DIY store to do it for you. I needed four long strips to go across the entire width of the wall, two long strips to go down the sides of the wall, then five medium strips for the large centre panels and ten short strips for the smaller, squarer panels.

- **Prepare your wall** by making sure it is as clean, dry and smooth as it can be, using sugar soap and sandpaper.

- **Fix the first panel strip to the wall**. I started with the panel strip that runs horizontally across the top of the wall, just below the ceiling. To make sure it was completely horizontal, I used a spirit level. My ceiling and wall were not straight at all so I had to make sure this top panel strip was dead level, so all the other panel strips worked around it, sitting either parallel or perpendicular to it. This was the most important strip and needed to be absolutely right. I used No More Nails adhesive to hold the strip in place, applying it along the back of the strip and pressing it against the wall.

- **Glue the remaining outer strips** in place. Working at right angles to the first horizontal strip, I added the two two long vertical strips on the outer edges, followed by another long horizontal strip that sat just above the skirting board, again using a spirit level to check that everything was straight and level.

- **Leave the glue to dry**. Because my wall was bowed rather than straight, after sticking the strips down, I leant some heavy shelving up against the strips to keep them in place. I left the shelving there for a good few hours until I was sure the glue had dried, so that added to the time this project took.

- **Add the remaining panel strips** to fill in the outer framework. I kept working down towards the floor, fixing the next two horizontal strips in place, carefully measuring the space between the panels. Lastly, I followed with all the vertical strips.

- **Use nails to hold the panel strips in place**, if necessary. My wall was so uneven that, as well as using No More Nails, I had to secure the central panel strips by tapping in some nails, so they didn't pop up again. I covered the nails by hanging a gold mirror (bought from Amazon) that matched the light fittings, but you can always use caulk and paint to cover up the nail heads.

- **Use caulk to fill any gaps**, if you have them. Across my wall, there were quite a few gaps and cracks, including a big one along the top. I used decorator's caulk to fill the gaps and then had to wait for it all to dry, so this stage took some time.

- **Leave everything to dry** before you even think about painting.

 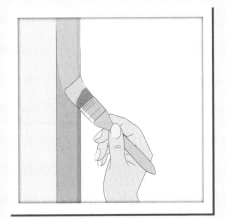

How to

USE A SPIRIT LEVEL

For loads of things, I just go for it and don't worry about using a spirit level but, for the panelling in this room I had to use a spirit level to make sure the panel strips were straight. Spirit levels, sometimes called bubble levels, will have a transparent vial in the middle almost completely filled with liquid, except for one bubble of air. You can choose from loads of different sizes and lengths, to make sure you get the most accurate result for your project. They can be bought pretty cheaply, with some models under £10.

❦ Place the spirit level in the centre of what you are trying to straighten. Make sure it is free of dirt, or anything else that might throw you off finding the right level. For me, I had to measure the first piece of panelling at the top. This needed to be right, so the rest of the panelling was correct.

❦ Once it is completely level, the bubble will sit in the middle of the two marks. If it sits to the left-hand side, that means the left hand is too high, and the right is too high if the bubble sits on the right-hand side.

❦ Make sure your eyes are level with the spirit level. You might need to crouch down or get on your tiptoes.

❦ Most spirit levels will also have two separate vials on each side to help you find vertical straight lines. Some more specialist tools will even help you find 45 degrees.

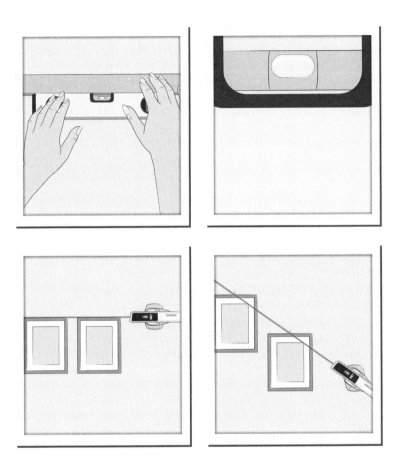

For some projects, I use a laser level. This tool projects a light onto the surface that you are trying to straighten out; this can be either a horizontal or vertical line (or even a diagonal). The line will stay projected there for when you are doing your work; this makes it a bit easier than holding a spirit level at the same time that you are trying to fix the thing that needs to be level. I often think how good it would be if I had eight arms like an octopus. I would be living the DIY dream! If you are renovating an entire house, I would invest in both a laser level and a spirit level to make your life easier.

UPCYCLING A CHEST OF DRAWERS

While I was waiting for the panel strips to dry on the wonky wall, I decided to think about paint colours for the room. At the same time, I wanted to upcycle some of Rex's old stuff. I felt like I had only just had him and so I was determined to use whatever I could again. Because I was pregnant, I was worried about using the right paint. I researched loads of paints and everyone said Farrow & Ball was a good safe brand. It is blimmin' expensive but they have an amazing palette of colours. For this one room, I decided to go all out.

I think Farrow & Ball paint is brilliant; it goes on really well and provides great coverage, but even the tester pots were expensive. I knew I wanted to use more than one shade of pink (the panelled wall was going to be a darker colour than the other walls), so I needed to make sure that they worked together. It wasn't like the conservatory or the Blue Loo, where I picked one shade and immediately loved it, job done. I bought four tester pots and after trying them out on the nursery walls, I used them to jazz up Rex's old chest of drawers. I wasn't wasting any of the testers – that would really cheese me off!

𝒱 First, I took the drawers out of the chest and removed the handles.

𝒱 Then I gave them a clean, followed by a light hand-sand using a bit of sandpaper to roughen up the surface. Remember to focus on the the front of the chest of drawers, where you will be painting.

𝒱 I painted the front side of the three drawers, each in a different shade of pink. I painted an undercoat

followed by a topcoat. I'm glad I did two coats, as a couple of the pinks were a bit purple at first.

𝒱 Joe then sealed the painted drawers with sealing spray and we left everything to dry completely. These types of sealers work a bit like a top coat for your nail polish – they protect the pretty paint finish from stains and chips. I always use a sealer spray when using chalk paint. There are different ways to apply sealants – a paintbrush or an applicator sponge – but I find a spray the easiest to use. Always spray evenly and resist the urge to touch your painted surface until the sealant is completely dry.

♥ I bought some new cute handles from Amazon and attached them to the drawers using the existing holes. You may need to enlarge the holes but mine fitted perfectly!

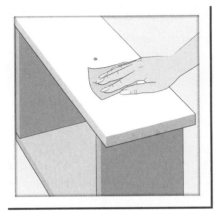

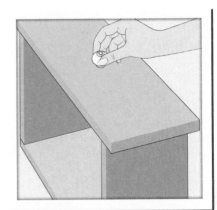

It made me so happy I could re-use Rex's chest of drawers. Baby furniture can be expensive, so it's nice that his little sister gets to make use of it. That makes me feel so good. You can absolutely transform any item of furniture and it just goes to show how far some £5 tester pots and £1.50 door handles will go!

The revamped chest of drawers went into the fitted cupboard in the corner of the nursery because I needed all the floor space and it would give me the room to have a chair. It was a bit tight but my dad helped me make enough space to wedge the chest of drawers in there and it fitted perfectly.

As well as painting the chest of drawers, I tried the testers out on loads of accessories, like little shelves, flamingo ornaments, and a couple of vases. I used those tester pots all up to the very last drop! All this helped me to decide on the best two shades for Rose's nursery – 'Nancy's Blushes' for the panelled wall and 'Middleton Pink' for the other walls.

HIRE A HOOVER

If you are doing big jobs in the house, always hire an industrial vacuum cleaner. It is so worth it. We hired one from Robert Dyas and used it for anything where there was loads of debris and mess. Give it some nails, screws and bits of wood, and even paint, and it loves it. It would be too much for poor Henry – he doesn't need a nail up his hose! So, when we rip up a carpet or sand a floor, I'll always give it a good heavy-duty hoovering.

COLOUR MATCH FOR CHEAPER PAINT

If you love a shade from one of the more expensive paint brands, you can try to colour match it with a cheaper paint at any DIY store. If you are struggling to find paint in a particular colour you absolutely love, you can also take in a flat, dry picture of that colour and they will scan and match it for you. You can even take a small sample home with you to check how it looks in different lights.

FLOWER WALL WITH MIRROR

On a trip to IKEA, I saw their flower wall displays and thought they were so beautiful. I wanted something similar in this room. For a second, I wondered whether it would be too much, and then I thought: no! If you love it, just do it. Basically, if I didn't have to share with Joe, I would have a flower wall in my own bedroom. I don't care if it's too much. I just couldn't help myself. I might be blowing my own trumpet here, but when I saw the finished effect, it was like the best thing I had ever seen! I'm so glad that I did it.

Before I created the flower wall, I sourced a mirror for the nursery. Mirrors in small rooms make a massive difference: they open the space up and make it look bigger and brighter. I needed to find something quite ornate to go with the style of the room and ended up choosing an overmantel mirror, even though there isn't a fireplace in this room. It was the style I was looking for, and looked almost like a window. I then bought my fake flower panels from a company called The Cheshire Gift Company; I had used them in my old house and I love the quality of their silk flowers.

♥ Decide where to hang your mirror. Once you've picked the spot, make sure that you don't make a hole where there are electric cables. These run up and down from light switches. As I mentioned before, there are cable detector tools that are designed to locate metals and live wires. They are relatively cheap and definitely worth the money. You just run the device over the area and it will beep if there is a cable behind the wall. Some styles flash red when there are cables or have a traffic-light system. Familiarise yourself with whatever style you are using, but these are a must-have.

♥ Secure your mirror on the wall using the right tools. Most mirrors come with D-rings and a cord, so attach the cord around the D-rings with a tight knot. If there is a metal cable, make sure you secure it by threading the cable through the D-rings and winding it together by at least 5cm. For mirrors, I always use two heavy-duty screws with rawl plugs in the wall to ensure they are really secure and the mirror can be hung evenly. Some mirrors come with serrated edges (use screws and rawl plugs) or strap hangers and J-hooks (hooks shaped like a J).

❦ Calculate how many flower panels you need. Once I deducted the space taken up by the mirror from my measurements, I needed ten flower panels to cover the wall.

❦ Fix the first flower panels to the wall. I started just above the skirting board, placing panels across the wall, and then worked upwards. First, I nailed the panels to the wall at the corners, and then staple-gunned any loose parts. As the flowers stand proud from the wall, you can't see any of the fixings.

❦ Work around your mirror or any other features. When I reached the mirror, I trimmed the panels to fit around the frame. Using my glue gun, I stuck some spare individual flowers into the decorative spaces in the frame so they fitted snugly and looked as though the flowers were growing through the frame.

❦ Trim the panels for a neat finish. Where the panels weren't an exact fit, I trimmed away the excess along the edges with a craft knife so they were straight and neat.

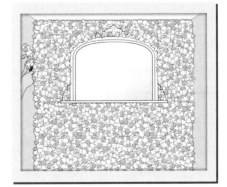

FURNITURE FOR DIFFERENT USES

For Rose's nursery, I bought an IKEA TV unit to store nappies, wipes, and creams, and some extra storage, instead of spending hundreds of pounds on a baby-changing unit. I'm not sure if I am the only terrible parent around, but one second my baby can't roll and the next they are doing handstands off the unit, so this time I decided to go for one that is low down, which would be safer. It means I can sit on the floor and change my baby – I'm lazy and love to sit down to do everything. It also meant that I could use the area under the window, which would otherwise just be dead space.

So I bought the TV unit and put it together myself. It was a bit of a sweaty job. I'm not going to lie, a couple of the panels were 100 per cent back to front but I managed to get it together. I changed the handles, using some floral rose handles from a small business called Swans and Bluebells, and added a changing wedge with a floral muslin covering from The Little House of Rainbows.

Using furniture for a different function from its original role is always a good idea. It's only a TV unit because the retailer calls it that. This doesn't apply only to baby stuff; you can use any piece of furniture however you want to!

RIP UP A CARPET

The carpet in the Rose's nursery was truly gross. Before we started decorating, we ripped it up so that the new floor could be laid. If you have someone coming in to lay your floor, they can remove the old carpet for you. Most flooring companies offer this service for a fee but we knew we could do it ourselves to save money.

- To detach the old carpet from the gripper rods that keep it in place along the walls, you just have to rip the carpet off of these strips. Starting in one corner and using pliers, simply pull. Gripper rods are strips of wood studded with tacks that go around the perimeter of the room and hold the edges of the carpet in place.

- Once you have prised the first corner of carpet up, you can then grab it and yank hard to pull it away from rest of the wall.

- Be careful of your fingers and wear protective gloves if you have them. You may want to cut the carpet into small sections as you go, using a utility knife.

- The same applies to any carpet underlay. Most are fixed in place using staples, so you will need to get these up. If any staples remain, just remove them using a staple remover.

- Some underlay is held in place with gripper rods. If you're fitting a new carpet you can leave these in place. If you're having hard flooring put down you will need to remove these gripper rods, using a crowbar.

LED Rose Light

On a trip to IKEA, I picked up a few bits because I wanted to make a special light for my little princess. I bought some fake roses, a string of battery-operated LED lights, and a stand with a glass casing for them to go in. I made this during a day when the boys were playing in their rooms, Rex was having a nap, and it was pouring with rain outside. I felt so anxious, so I decided to get out my glue gun and get crafting. While I was pregnanrt, I would switch this light on and off again. I would feel so excited, with genuine butterflies, at how eager I was to meet my baby girl.

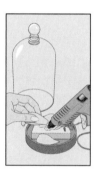

STEP 1   STEP 2   STEP 3   STEP 4

- ❦ **DISMANTLE THE ROSE** partially by removing a few outer petals.

- ❦ **COVER THE BATTERY** unit with those petals using a glue gun.

- ❦ **THREAD THE LED LIGHTS** through the rose, then re-assemble it.

- ❦ **GLUE THE ROSE** to the base, standing it upright, coil the remaining LED lights inside the glass casing, before closing it.

Little things I love ♡

SPECIAL HANGERS FOR BABY CLOTHES

The reality of baby clothes is that you change your little one around four times a day because they are continually being sick and pooing on everything. You need a lot of babygrows, which you want to be able to access quickly from handy drawers. But you will also have a few special baby clothes, maybe an outfit for a christening or a wedding. I say go all out and put those clothes on display on special hangers. Your baby will probably only wear them once, but if you can show them off, then at least they will look beautiful! On my show Sort Your Life Out, we never throw anything away; at one house, there were these vintage floral fabric hangers, which I loved and I used them here.

DON'T PANIC

The most important thing with any new baby isn't having a state-of-the-art nursery; it is getting the right support in place, which will help you feel calm. Having a new-born is overwhelming and exhausting, and it is just so important to have the right people around you. With my little girl, Rose, my top priorities were making sure I had booked a slot with the perinatal mental health support team and getting a breastfeeding specialist in straight away to help me. Those two things were far more important than having the right furniture in the nursery.

For the first six months your baby isn't going anywhere, so if you are preparing a nursery, don't panic about getting it all done straight away, or buying every piece of equipment immediately. You could end up needing everything in the baby shop or absolutely nothing. For example, you might want to breastfeed and find you can't, so you then need a steriliser, bottles, and formula.

I only bought a few babygrows, a pack of nappies, and some other small bits and pieces, and then decided to buy whatever else I needed after Rose had arrived. If you are on a budget, there are also loads of great groups and sites for pre-loved baby clothes. As for storage, I was lucky that I had a nursery room to work with. When Rex was a baby, he just had a tiny section of my own wardrobe and we made do with that.

FLOORING

The only expert help I had in this room was for the flooring. When we took the old carpet up, the underlay had some very weird stains. Ribena? Who knows! Once it was up, they plied the floor to make it straight, which wasn't the easiest task as the room is not very straight!

Again, I chose a pretty white herringbone laminate. It made sense to go for a hard floor because I knew if the baby made a mess, I could just get my mop out! I couldn't resist having a go when the flooring team was laying it – it is a bit like doing a jigsaw! Once it was done, I felt like I could cry. The original floor had been so disgusting, but once it was up the room felt so much bigger and cleaner.

PICKLE COTTAGE

The Utility Room

I was determined to build a functional utility room that is an extension of our kitchen. I wanted the room to be as big and practical as possible, to make our day-to-day lives easier.

As well as having space for me to tackle my horrendous, never-ending laundry pile, I wanted a room with enough space for all the kids' bags and shoes, and for the animals and all their stuff.

The hallway in Pickle Cottage was so big, we were able to borrow some space to create the utility room. When building the room, I wanted a wall with a soft, curved corner because it is the first thing you see when you come down the stairs. Plus the kids are always running down the stairs, so I wanted it to be as safe as possible. I can't tell you how many builders told us we couldn't have a curved wall as it was simply not a thing. Well, it is a thing! The whole cottage has curves – they are everywhere in our home. I knew it was harder work and people didn't want to do it but I kept saying 'It can be done!' When you are renovating somewhere you might be forever, there is no point compromising. You have to be confident and strong, and don't let anyone talk you out of it. I didn't want to be looking at the wall of my utility room every day, thinking, 'I wish I had just done what I wanted.' Eventually, a builder put in my dream wall.

I asked the company that fitted the units to keep the original wooden beams in this room as I love them. The installation of the units by Wren Kitchens went so well we chose to use them again for our kitchen. Because they fitted out the utility room first, I got an impression of how they worked. They kept to their deadlines and budget, and were easy to work with. They listened to what I was saying and carefully cut the units around the exposed beams. I was SO happy with the result.

I am not sure how I chose the green colour! The kitchen company gave us a massive colour chart, and it sounds so sad but I was trying to get the tones of my first Tap to Tidy book, with the eucalyptus on the front. It makes me feel so calm and bright. There are no windows in the utility room so I knew I wanted a pale colour but I also wanted something that stood out. At that stage, I already had blue, purple, pink, black and white, and I thought, 'What else do I need? Green!'

I decided to get a professional tiler in to complete the tiling and sink splashback. Would I do tiling myself? Yes, I would. If any tiling was needed in Rex's room, I would give it a go because I've done everything in that room and don't mind the odd mistake. If you are getting brand-new kitchen units in a room, looking at the cupboards against wonky tiling could be quite upsetting. If you are inexperienced at tiling, the end result won't be perfect. It only took a tiler a day to lay these tiles, so it wasn't a huge expense and looks immaculate. I'm delighted.

USE ALL THE SPACE

I really wanted to use absolutely every inch of storage space in the utility room. In one corner of the room, we have some shoe cubby holes and I didn't want the corner to be boxed off, so I now have a hidden space for wellies and umbrellas in a plastic bucket, and the cover lifts up. The whole area looks like a seating area but if you lift the cushion, there is a secret world underneath!

I also wanted tall cupboard spaces. In the kitchen, I planned to have fewer high cabinets, so I put all my 'overflow' stuff from the kitchen here, like my baking stuff, which I use less often. I don't think it makes sense in the kitchen to be wading through cake tins to get to your everyday saucepans, so if you have the luxury of keeping stuff elsewhere, definitely do it.

I also put some of my crafting bits, like my glue gun, scissors, and string in here, so I don't need to keep going down to the shed all the time to fetch them when inspiration strikes!

It is always, always a good idea to have a tall cupboard for the mop and hoover. Mops are the ugliest thing ever and a hoover stand is always worth the investment. You drill it to the wall and everyone knows where to put the bloomin' hoover back! Everything can stay together and then you can shut the door and you don't have to look at it. Winning!

How to

MAKE LAUNDRY EASIER

If you are going to be doing loads of laundry and have the space, make sure you have an area for storing the dirty washing. I knew I had the space to have a hidden drawer for my laundry. Why have a laundry basket on view when you can keep the mess out of sight? They asked me if I wanted a rubbish bin in one of the units but I asked for laundry bins instead. Now the unit that we have for laundry is where the bin unit would be and has two main buckets – one for darks, one for lights – and then another couple of smaller ones, that I use for delicates and socks. We lose all our flippin' socks!

We are lucky to have space for a separate washer and dryer but I have also used combination washer/dryers and I think they are really good. Generally, I try not to use my dryer too much because I think that clothes last longer when they dry naturally. I always try to dry stuff outside whenever I can because I like the fresh smell the washing gets (and it saves on energy bills!). Using the tumble dryer is more of an emergency thing for me, and for thick and heavy materials or bedding that is not going to dry easily. I also hang up my stuff as soon as it comes out the washer as I think it dries better. Even the bigger stuff, like sheets, Joe and I will shake out and straighten before we hang them over the drying rack.

When we first moved into Pickle Cottage and the electricity bills were so high, I called the electricity company and they advised that I do all my washing at night because it is cheaper. I tend to do two loads a day and sit in the utility room when the kids are in bed. If there is stuff that's dried, I will fold it and put it away, so there is nothing to do in the morning. It feels quite cathartic.

MAKE A HOUSE FOR THE ANIMALS

When I created the utility room, it doubled as the best bedroom for our dogs, Peanut and Theo. Because the floor is tiled, we can easily keep it clean. My dogs love being cosy and in their own spot and they also like noise, so they love the tumble dryer going, or the fridge humming! It's also a lovely warm room. I dedicated two spaces for them and their little dog beds. There are two compartments above each space for their food bowls to be stored and then there are separate drawers for their leads, clothes, and any other little accessories. Sadly we lost Theo soon after creating this room, but I feel happy she got to spend time in here and was part of our lives at Pickle Cottage. She was the best little dog and a friend to us all. She bought so much love into our lives.

THINK ABOUT THE LIGHTING

We really needed to think carefully about the lighting in this room because there are no windows in there. We had downlights in the ceiling, but I would also say to always get under-cabinet lighting. Our surfaces here are a pale colour, so they reflect light and it makes the space feel really welcoming.

ALWAYS FIT EXTRA SOCKETS

If you're having units fitted, always get extra sockets inside for charging up devices. If you have cupboard space (especially if it is away from the main kitchen) use that space to charge up your tablets and phones. These tend to always end up on the kitchen surface and sometimes I think it just looks so messy! I've made sure there are loads of sockets in the utility cupboards so that we can hide stuff away.

Little things I love ♡

COMPACT IRONING BOARD

I hate ironing, and getting the ironing board out is such a faff! I was thinking about getting a pull-out one when my dad found this amazing compact ironing board from Joseph Joseph. It wasn't cheap, although it was around the same price as a normal ironing board. The board itself folds out and it has little legs to stand on a tabletop so you can iron on any surface. It takes two seconds to put up. I know we are so lucky to have this space but it would work just as well on any kitchen worktop or even on the floor. It's so cute and convenient and I'm not constantly grappling with a massive ironing board.

I also plan to have a rail where I can hang up shirts. I wash the boys' school shirts and put them on a spin, so the moisture is out of them but instead of putting them in the tumble dryer, I hang them up straight away to dry on a hanger, and they mostly dry without creases, so I'm not ironing a million and one school shirts a week.

Upcycling Bottles for Detergent and Softener

I first had large Kilner jars with pouring taps in the pink utility room of my old house. Even though they are meant for drinks, they are perfect for dispensing laundry detergent and softener. Originally I spray painted them pink to fit in with the colour scheme of that room. I really didn't want to get rid of them, so I decided to upcycle them instead.

◊ **CHOOSE YOUR PAINT**. Originally I painted the jars using spray paint and did two coats and then a sealant. I wish I'd done three coats as they were still a bit transparent! This time I used standard emulsion paint that matched the room the best. I was quite far along in my pregnancy, so I felt that was the safest option. I literally painted on a couple of coats and left them in the sun to dry.

◊ **ADD A LID**. I don't know about you but I am always left with loads of spare lids from Tupperware, so I decided to use two wooden lids for the jars to match the wood in other parts of the room. I think they look better.

◊ **FIX YOUR LABELS.** I added sticky labels to each jar. I always use labels from my sister's company, The Label Lady.

I have loads of pink plastic storage tubs from my old utility room. Rather than buying new ones, I am going to get Joe to spray-paint them green. I am also reusing all of my old baskets because... why not? You don't need to buy new every time you change colour scheme. Even at Christmas, I spray all my baubles. If I want to go yellow next year, I can! You can also paint any fitted units and it instantly gives your room a fresh new look.

BUY IN BULK

I always try to buy eco-friendly brands like Method, Ecover and Bio-D. We have a septic tank at the cottage, so we have to be careful about what we are using because our waste water goes into the ground, but eco-friendly products are better for the environment all round. By buying in bulk, it means there is less packaging, we are doing fewer trips to the shops, and it works out cheaper in the long-run. Buying lots of smaller bottles does make it more expensive for eco-friendly products. But if you have the space to store bigger quantities of stuff like washing detergent and cleaning fluid, it is always worth it. If you don't have space to buy in bulk, try shopping at a zero-waste store where you can refill old containers.

You also need to prioritise: would you like five bottles of multi-purpose cleaner or a large one that you can use to refill a smaller bottle? If buying five bottles makes you happy, then do it, but I don't believe that you need to spend more money and loads of space to be eco friendly with cleaning products.

MAKE IT LIGHT!

I think when you walk into your home, the most important thing is to make it bright, light, and airy. I painted our hall white for a completely fresh space.

Little things I love

LOCKABOX

I don't know about anyone else but when my kids were younger, they were obsessed with Calpol. They would always try to get hold of it, so I bought this box to store all our medicines. It has a number-code combination lock at one end, so no one is getting in there unless they know the code. We use ours to keep all our regular medicines, like Calpol, ibuprofen, and antihistamines in. And the plasters – Rex loves the plasters! I keep trying to tell him they are not stickers!

MAKE IT FUN FOR THE KIDS

It's so hard when you have a mountain of laundry to wash and you also want to occupy and play with your kids. My advice is this: bring your kids in there with you and get them to 'help' you by using their own kit. In a cupboard in my utility room, Rex has his own mini washing machine, brush, and cleaning gear. I also think by occupying kids like this you can stop them from trying to get into the other cupboards. I think restricting kids from all the cupboards makes them a bit crazy and think whatever is inside must be very exciting. It's like Pandora's Box!

I put all the dangerous stuff, like bleach and dishwasher tablets, in the high cupboards and I put some magnetic locks on some of the other doors – the ones that contain surface sprays and other risky cleaning materials. Aside from the safety element, I don't need Rex messing up my room by pouring washing-up liquid all over the floor, because this is totally what he would do!

Seasonal Slab

Throughout the year, I always decorate a seasonal slab. It all started when I had a slab of wood that I sanded down and then put a few pretty flowers on. That was my springtime slab. When summer came around, I put some more seasonal stuff on the slab that made me smile. Now I try to do one every season. Often I use the same bits and pieces each year, or occassionally add the odd new thing.

V **FIND YOUR SLAB**. This can be an offcut of wood leftover from a DIY project, an old piece of driftwood washed up on a beach, or a plank from your own garden. Or you can buy something new. If the wood is rough, sand it down.

V **DECORATE YOUR SLAB**.
I put things on my seasonal slab that simply make me happy. My autumn slab has a vase filled with pampas grass, cotton plants, and eucalyptus from Primark. Then I added my little gnome – his name is Norm and he comes from a small business called Pretty Little Home. You all know how I feel about Norms, and that I can never have too many! My final addition was an LED pumpkin light from Lights4Fun. These little things bring me joy!

Little things I love ♡

PERSONALISED SHELF

The main shelf above the sink in the utility room is a floating shelf that I fixed to the wall like any other floating shelves. Ours has 'Pickle Cottage' carved into it. If it's your forever home, you put that name everywhere. It means that when I see it, I know that it is in my space, my world, my home. This was from one of my favourite small businesses, Fall With Grace. Later on, I also added a personalised house name sign to our gate (also from Fall With Grace) and it looks so special!

On my shelf, I put another cute little gnome and an apple and a pear from Pretty Little Home. When I first started putting things on the shelf, I was so emotional, and it made me feel like the room was really coming together.

CHANGE A FUSE

If an electrical item has given up, it might mean that you need to change the fuse in the plug. The fuse is a really important component used in electric circuits and it's designed to switch off the current when problems occur, to stop any further damage. When fuses blow, they will need to be replaced. It's easier than you think.

- First things first. Always switch off and unplug any electrical items before doing any maintenance.

- Unscrew the cover of the plug in an anticlockwise direction and remove it. Some plugs might have a fuse cover or pop-out fuse holder and you may need to use a slightly smaller flathead screwdriver to get it off.

- Take out the old fuse using a screwdriver; sometimes they are a bit stiff to get out. Replace the fuse.

- Make sure you are switching it for a fuse with the right amperage. Items like microwaves, kettles, and toasters and appliances over 700w need a 13A fuse whilst lamps and mixers and appliances up to 700w need a 3A fuse. Always check what it says on the manufacturers' instructions. Basically, I always change one fuse for the same type and amperage.

- Return the cover to the plug and screw on firmly. There should be no movement and the plug should fit firmly into the wall.

- If you are ever worried about the electrics, or if changing the fuse hasn't fixed the problem, or if your fuses are blowing a lot, call an electrician in to check that everything is working as it should.

DON'T LET THE HALLWAY
BECOME A DUMPING GROUND

When you are creating a communal space near the front door, try to make an organised area for the stuff that bugs you. I think every busy house has to have a 'system' that the kids know, so no one is falling over school bags, rucksacks, and other stuff all the time, losing their school blazers or coats, or generally not knowing where their things are. When everything is dumped on the floor and the kids just kick their shoes off, it is so annoying!

You have to have a strict code of conduct with it, too. When the boys come through the door, they will now hang their coats up, put their shoes in a cubby hole and their bags in a labelled box. They have to stick to it whether they like it or not. If they don't, then their stuff can be put outside to be rained on. I'm not having a situation where I am breaking my neck tripping over their stuff, and no one knows where anything is. Things are hectic on school days: I do a packed lunch for Leighton and Rex, and there are three different school runs – we drop Zachary and Leighton at different schools and then Rex at his nursery, so they have to be organised as we don't have the time in the morning for them to lose their shoes and coats!

Our space is a luxury and we are so privileged, but even before we had this, we have always had a clear section in the house for shoes, and they do not go anywhere else. The kids have to take their shoes off when they come in.

Expert Help ♡

SANDBLASTING WOODWORK
IN THE HALLWAY

Our old wooden stairs are so charming and I love
the detailing on them, but they were dark and covered
in red carpet, and it made them feel really closed in.
So we ripped the carpet up and stripped the wood back
to its original colour.

The stairs and some of the beams have some pretty
delicate moulding. Ours had been painted black
(goodness knows how many moons ago) and I knew
it would not be an easy job stripping off the paint. So
we got a company in to sandblast all the beams, stairs,
some flooring, and other woodwork. A sandblaster is a
machine that uses sand or broken-up glass to blast away
paint, varnish, or rust (if you are sandblasting metal).

If it was a smaller area I would have done it myself, one million per cent, pregnant or not; I'd have put on my goggles and mask and just got on with it. In this case, we needed all the beams in the whole house sandblasted and there was so much that needed doing that it was worth paying for someone to come in and do it for us. It cost £1,000, which I know is a huge amount of money but, it felt like an investment, and afterwards the beams looked completely different.

If I was sandblasting a smaller piece of wood or furniture, I would probably hire a sandblaster. What is important with this kind of work is to get a bit of practice with sandblasting, so you can get a real feel for it (there is not much room for error). One thing I would say is that it is VERY messy and dusty. Joe was not happy, and said it was like living on a beach as there was so much sand everywhere!

Wood has different grains and irregularities like knots, so it might look quite different after it's been sandblasted. There were various types of wood underneath our paint; there was pine, mahogany, and two different types of oak. I didn't want to get rid of it because I love wood. If it had been all one colour I would've stained it. It is also OK to leave the wood raw. However, all the woods are so different that the plan is to paint it all one colour. At the time of writing, I am planning to sand it down by hand, change all the skirting (because it's uneven), and then paint it all a fresh white. I need to make time for this, as I know it won't be a quick job. I feel that realistically it would take about three weeks to complete.

Then I want a runner up the stairs. This is a slim carpet that is fitted in the middle of the stairs. It brings the warmth and colour of a carpet whilst still showing the woodwork either side.

PAINTING A CABINET

In our hallway was a pretty old cabinet built into the wall. I knew that I wasn't going to store anything of use in there but I wanted to show it off because it was so ornamental, so I decided to give it a new lease of life. When I was upcycling it, my grandma had gone into a care home, and I planned to put some of her things in there, so it would become filled with special memories of her.

♥ Empty the cabinet, clean it inside and out, and ensure it's dry.

♥ Take out any inside shelving and unscrew any handles. This piece of furniture had two glass shelves that I removed, and cleaned, so I could paint inside.

♥ Lightly sand the area and brush away any dust.

♥ I used a white 'one coat' emulsion paint on both the inside and outside of the cabinet but it needed a couple of coats, to be honest, because the wood was so dark.

♥ If you are tackling a cabinet like this you might want to tape up the glass areas. For me, the easiest way is to paint really carefully and quickly run a damp cloth over any mistakes before the paint dries.

♥ Leave everything to dry before putting any shelving back in and the handles back on.

♥ I scrubbed the handles to clean them, but they were not brass and they peeled. Joe ended up spray-painting them black for me and they looked really good against the white.

Pumpkin Flower Pot

Once the cabinet was finished, I put a side table in front of it and decided to upcycle some of last year's (artificial) pumpkins. These came from Pretty Little Home. Rex and I spent a couple of happy hours in the sun painting together. It makes me so ridiculously happy that he will still do this with me even though the older two have well and truly grown out of it! Once they were dry, and while Rex was having a nap, I decided to create a little flower pot.

STEP 1   STEP 2   STEP 3   STEP 4

𝒱 **SLICE OFF THE TOP** of a large polystyrene pumpkin, then paint the flat area. Leave it to dry completely.

𝒱 **INSERT SOME DRIED FLOWERS** into the pumpkin by poking the stems into the flat part. My flowers were all orange shades and came from ByBonhomie. If the stems are not strong enough to pierce the polystyrene, make a small hole first with a bradawl or skewer.

𝒱 **ARRANGE YOUR PUMPKIN** to make a display. You could also add some smaller pumpkins around the main pumpkin, like I did!

𝒱 **ENJOY YOUR DISPLAY!** Mine gave me absolute life!

Quick fix

PAINTING AN ARCH ON A WALL

I had seen so many people paint arches on walls and they looked so brilliant, I decided to have a go. The great thing about doing painting yourself, is that if it looks awful you can paint right over it.

- To make the shape, I measured my wall and then found the centre and put a nail into it.

- Then I found the radius of the circle I wanted for the curve of the arch, and tied one end of a piece of string to a pencil and the other end to the nail so that they were the radius's length apart. (Cut the string slightly longer than the radius to allow for tying it to the pencil and the nail, and double check your measurements.)

- Pull the string tight to make your semi-circle so you maintain equal distance from the nail as you make the shape.

- Once you have your semi-circle in place, mark the vertical sides

of the arch straight down from the semi-circle. Tape around the outside of the arch so you can paint the inside. Use Frog Tape if you have it – when I did ours, I only had regular masking tape.

- Paint your arch. In fact, I found it easier to paint the curve without the tape – it just gave me a false sense of security and I wasn't as careful. I used some Farrow & Ball paint in 'Jitney' that we had left over from doing our bedroom.

- Add your floating shelf. Rex screwed the nails in for ours!

- Once your shelf is up, add accessories. I added some pampas grass in a little vase, a buddha, and a candle.

The Bedroom

♡

I wanted our bedroom to be a sanctuary and place of relaxation for just Joe and me. (And the baby for a bit!) It's such a bright and light space but I also wanted it to feel cosy and calm.

As much as I long for our bedroom to be a place for just Joe and I, the reality is that it is often a room for all! It will always hold a special place in my heart, because it was where Rose was born.

There's no right way or wrong way to give birth, but I can honestly say I've never felt so calm and relaxed being in my own home. I've always associated birth with trauma and I have felt really scared when I go into labour and being in hospital almost confirms that fear. Being at home made me feel so much more in control. Rose was born on my birthday and was the best present. It is also the place where the boys met her for the first time and it was just magical. Rose's cot is currently in this bedroom but when she is old enough, she will move into her nursery.

I always try to have a few moments to myself whenever I can, so sometimes I sneak up to use the rolltop bath in our bedroom when the kids are being looked after. When this happens and I get to take a relaxing bath on my own, I feel like I have won a competition! I shut my eyes and enjoy every second until all hell breaks loose again! This is normally the kids running in followed by Peanut and Teddy who have their favourite spot on the chair.

How to

USE POSH PAINT

It's really important to love the colour of your bedroom because it's the first thing you see when you wake up every morning and the last thing you look at before going to sleep each night. There are some rooms that you can paint and think, 'It's not my favourite shade, but it'll do!' Your bedroom is not one of those rooms! Love your colour!

When I saw this paint colour – 'Jitney' from Farrow & Ball – I thought, 'That is it!' I tried to colour match that exact shade with other cheaper brands but I couldn't. It just didn't come out the same. In the end, we swallowed the extra cost as it is our bedroom and so somewhere that we didn't mind spending a little more on.

You have to find the right paint for you – and the right way to use it. When it comes to achieving a good finish, I think it is as much about how you apply the paint as the paint itself. You can have the poshest paint in the world but unless you apply it properly, it might still look a bit shit.

For large spaces, make sure you paint with long strokes. In some spaces and for more intricate jobs (windows, furniture etc.), it's important to make all the brush strokes in one direction. I enjoy some meticulous painting – I find it really therapeutic. Joe finds it mind-numbing; but, as much of a ball-ache as some of the slower painting jobs are, you have to get over it if you want it to look nice.

For the ceilings and walls of a room like this, I just whacked it on with the roller and it looked great. Joe also loves a slap-and-roll job!

Quick fix

FILLING A HOLE IN THE WALL

No matter how careful you are, there will inevitably come a time when you need to fill a hole in your wall. Some people seem to think it is a massive ordeal but I promise you that it isn't.

- Fill any small holes made by nails or screws, using a wall- or general-purpose filler. Apply firm pressure as you fill the hole.

- Level the surface of the filler by smoothing it off with a scraping tool. Try to make sure the filler is flush with the wall surface.

- Sand the filler down to give it a smooth finish, if necessary.

- Paint over the filled hole once the filler has dried completely. It really is that easy!

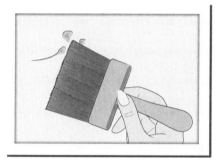

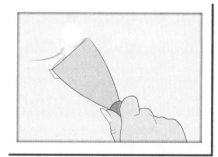

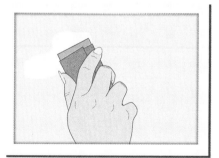

Little things I love ♡

THE FIREPLACE

I just love being cosy and knew I wanted some extra warmth in the bedroom. We bought our custom-made electric fire, which has a marble stone surround and mantelpiece, from Fireplace Factory. When I was expecting Rose I knew that I would be spending a lot of time breastfeeding and hibernating in my bedroom – the fire was an early birthday gift to myself so I could be extra toasty.

It has a remote control and you can change the colour of the flame – Rex thinks it is better than any TV channel! I put some white stones along the bottom where the flames appear to personalise the fire before the unit was sealed. I also love to decorate the fireplace with the changing seasons.

MAKE YOUR BED LOOK BEAUTIFUL

I love a neat and tidy bed. There is nothing more inviting at the end of the day than fresh, clean linens and crease-free pillows. Bliss! I like to use different bed linens depending on the seasons, so in spring and summer, I love cooler fabrics like linens and crumpled cotton, whereas in winter I am all about a teddy fleece or sheep skin throws for cosy warmth. I always choose textured bed linens that don't need to be ironed – whose got time for that? I simply dry them then pop them straight on the bed. No-fuss. (Or getting tangled up in loads of gigantic sheets!)

I make my bed by simply pulling everything off, smoothing out the sheets and wafting the duvet on top, followed by any blankets or throws. I put two sleeping pillows flat, then two more to the front along with any extra cushions. I tuck in my duvet, blankets and throws by using one end of a wooden hanger to flatten everything straight and tuck it in, so it looks smooth and ironed. Finally, I sit a wooden tray on the freshly made bed, with a scented candle, a few fejkas in a vase (no need to add water, so no chance of any spills) and my book. Easy!

Small Accessories That Make a Big Difference

When it comes to accessories, I try to work with what I already have, rather than buy anything new. I have reused a little mirror that came from our old house on one of the walls and I have brought out my swinger's grass and favourite candles to go on the shelves. All my indoor flowers and plants are either dried or fake. I call them fejkas, which is IKEA's name for their fake potted plants (see page 110). I would really, really love to be good with real potted plants but can barely keep my own kids alive so what chance would a plant stand!

For me, accessorising is about living my life, seeing something that I like and then incorporating it into my décor. It's not about going out specifically to shop for accessories or putting too much pressure on myself to fully accessorise a space straightaway. Just let the stuff come to you; let life guide you.

I prefer to arrange things in a group of three – some flowers, an ornament, and a candle on a shelf, for example. Or a picture, print or photo in a frame. I also like to take cheap picture frames and fill them with dried plant stems, such as bunny's tails and other fluffy grasses that I love. Here's what I did:

♥ **REMOVE THE EXISITING PICTURE** from the frame.

♥ **POSITION THE BUNNY'S TAIL**, grass or whatever else you want in your frame. You may need to hold it in position with a dab of glue.

♥ **CLOSE THE FRAME AND HANG THE PICTURE**. Sometimes I leave the backing card out of my frames, so the colour of the wall becomes part of the picture; this is an easy way of tying everything into the room.

Quick fix

CREATING A GALLERY WALL

Gallery walls are just an opportunity to create an area on your wall with a collection of pictures that you love, and there are no right or wrong choices. I think it is nice to create a cohesive colour palette; my bedroom gallery wall is based around the cream tones in the bedroom. Not everything needs to be art! On my bedroom wall, I have some dried grasses in frames too.

◊ Measure the available wall space and gather together all your favourite pictures.

◊ Lay out the pictures on the floor in the arrangement you think you might like on the wall, leaving gaps between the images for the frames. You might prefer neat rows or a more freeform arrangement.

◊ Select the main picture that you want to make the centre of attention. I always start in the middle with one of the bigger pictures and then work outwards from there.

◊ Combine vertical and horizontal images in a freeform arrangement as this helps to add a bit of variety and interest to the design.

◊ Stand back and look at the overall design. Keep moving the pictures around until you find the perfect arrangement that you like the best.

◊ Take a photo of every possible combination so that you can easily recreate the perfect one.

◊ Choose picture frames for each of the images. They can either blend in with the colour of the wall or stand out in contrast. All the picture frames could match in style and colour, or each one could be slightly different. You could gather together lots of frames in different styles and then spray paint them the same colour to tie everything together.

◊ Check you are happy with the final arrangement before making any holes in the wall. If the frames are not too heavy, sometimes I use Blu Tack to stick my pictures provisionally to the wall.

◊ Keep some spare frames in a mix of different sizes as you might want to chop and change the pictures over time.

CHOOSE FREE PRINTS

It can be fun decorating walls and letting your imagination run wild but you do not always have to buy prints. I wanted a theme of pictures with grasses that I love, like pampas grasses, and black-and-white buildings. You can just go onto Google and search for free prints and if you have a colour printer you can print them off.

There's some incredible photography out there that is high-quality and royalty-free. Make sure you download the highest resolution available because this will mean the clearest image and you may be able to increase the size of the picture if you need to. You can also print off pictures onto computer paper and use it as wrapping paper or for cards. I printed off the pictures and put them in IKEA frames.

CHECK OUT THE RULES ON DIY NOISE

I know it can be tempting to pick up the drill whenever the moment takes you and crack on with a DIY job but if it's late at night or on weekends, it is really important to check. Each local council will have rules around when you can make DIY noise and this will depend on where you live. Your local council should have a page on their website that will tell you exactly what you need to know. Some limit the use of power tools to three hours a day, whilst others might say that DIY should only be completed on a Sunday in an emergency.

With so many people now working from home, I think it's also a really good idea to let your neighbours know if you are planning on doing something particularly noisy and how long you think it is going to take, so they can plan around it.

ORGANISE HIS AND HERS WARDROBE SPACE

Give him one cupboard. That is what I have done, I am not even joking! In all honesty, in our dressing room area, we are lucky enough to have a side of our little room each – mine is the longest one, obviously! In the hanging areas, I colour-coordinate my clothes together on one side and Joe does the same on the other side. Everything is in colour order so we know where we will find each garment. When I am getting dressed in the morning, I don't think, 'What outfit will I wear today?' The majority of the time, I wonder, 'What colour will I wear today?'

In the drawers, I have my bulky items that take up too much space, like tracksuits, jeans, pyjamas, and underwear. That makes it easy to organise. I don't own loads and loads of shoes. Most of mine are slippers! I do have a shoe rack under one of the hanging spaces in my wardrobe. I don't think you can go wrong with this style because underneath the hanging space you can just fit a single shelf for shoes. It also stops you from collecting junk from downstairs and bunging it into the bottom of the wardrobe.

I think if you plan to get new fitted wardrobes, it is worth trying to allocate a space for make-up. I have dedicated space in our dressing room for my make-up and it's in front of the mirror, so I have loads of natural light to see what I am doing. There was an awkward corner so we created some shallow shelves in that space, and that is where my make-up lives. You really can make use out of even the most tricky spaces.

You can always be creative with bedroom storage. Even if you don't have space for a wardrobe, it is possible to make a place for clothes on a hanging rail. Clothes can look pretty when they are out and don't necessarily need to be hidden away.

LEARN HOW TO FOLD

I think one of the best things you can do to keep your bedroom tidy is learn how to fold. The Folding Lady on Instagram is a great place to start. She shows how to fold bedding, clothes, towels, and everything, so they look really neat and tidy. So even if you have to put stuff out on shelves, it looks really pretty.

Little things I love ♡

CHANDELIER PENDANT LIGHT

The dressing area is such a small space that
I wanted a light with some reflection on it to spread
the brightness around. I chose the chandelier light
from a company called Pagazzi Lighting, and it
has loads of crystal panels that bounce the light
around the room, which makes it look much bigger.
The pendant is long and thin because the room is
narrow and it works really well. You can adjust the
height of a chandelier – ours hangs only slightly
down from the ceiling. An electrician hung this
chandelier light for us. It feels so special and makes
the room a proper little sanctuary.

Little things I love ♡

MY SHEEP CHAIR

I bought this bouclé chair to sit at the dressing table and I have been so impressed with it. It is so fluffy with super-soft fibres – I think it feels like a sheep. It is really warming and cosy to sit on! I was after one of these chairs for ages but the posh brands cost anything from £300 upwards. Then I spotted the one I eventually bought, which was £89 from Homebase. It goes to show that it definitely does make sense to shop around and have a really good search online.

WHY CHOOSE CARPET?

Our little dressing area is the only room in the house where we have carpet. With kids, I think hard floors are much easier to clean and keep looking good. This is the one room they are not allowed in and they have no interest in coming in here either, so I decided to treat myself to some carpet. Everywhere else is wipe clean but in here I asked for the fluffiest, luxurious, most child-unfriendly carpet they had! It's cream and feels like the best ever. I could have a lie down on it!

Expert Help ♡

BEDROOM BATH

Baths are my absolute favourite thing. I have
always wanted my own luxury rolltop bath. Having
special baths and bath bombs just gives me life.
When we moved into this house, the bedroom had
a space that just felt a bit empty – there was no
wardrobe there and it was surrounded by windows.
Immediately, I said that 100 per cent I wanted a
bath in that spot. Loads of builders and plumbers
said it couldn't be done, but I found someone
who said that they could do it. In the end, it was
actually quite straightforward. There was already
hot water upstairs so they went into the loft and
chased the hot and cold water into the bedroom.

Then they put a hole through the wall for an outflow pipe. Everything here goes into the septic tank and the ground. The most awkward bit was putting the drain into the tank but it worked. It wasn't the impossible job that everyone else said it would be.

I bought a freestanding rolltop bath from the Cast Iron Bath Company. It was extremely heavy so I needed to check that the floor could take the weight of the bath before it was delivered. Luckily there are some heavy-duty strong joists in the cottage, otherwise we would have had to get someone in to reinforce the floor. The one thing I would recommend when getting something this heavy is: never ask for kerbside delivery! It took Joe, my brother-in-law, and the four men who were working on the utility room to get it up the stairs and into the bedroom. It was while I was shouting 'pivot' as they were trying to get it up our stairs that I knew they all hated me that day. It was so bad.

But I just adore my bath. I was able to choose my own colours, taps, plugs, and everything, and it is one of the most beautiful baths that I have ever seen. I love it so much that, when it was first installed, I even considered giving birth in it! It's where I wanted to be!

I placed a ladder shelf (see page 136) next to the bath, from the Garden Trading Company, with plants and other bath stuff on it and the whole thing looks so pretty. We also had flooring fitted by a local flooring company, A Clarke Carpets & Flooring.

The
Kitchen

♡

Our kitchen was the last room we tackled during the renovations. This part of our project ran a bit later than we had wanted for various reasons – not least the arrival of Rose!

I think with any renovations, you need to accept that delays are inevitable, other stuff will happen and things might not always run completely to plan. It is always worth it though. Watching our kitchen finally come together feels amazing. I am so grateful and excited.

The kitchen was overall the biggest job we tackled as we not only completely replaced the old units but also added a small extension on the side of the cottage to make the room squarer. As well as building the extension, we also put in new glazing with large windows and bifold doors to make the kitchen feel much bigger and brighter.

Fortunately this work didn't require planning permission, however, we did need to check that the work fell under Permitted Development (these are rights that allow you to build up to a certain size without planning permission).

I know some people will think that because I am in the public eye, trades and other companies will feel they have to do a really good job when they do work on my house. Actually, they don't. I can assure you that we've had workers who have left halfway through the job, or that have not turned up when they said they would.

There are people out there who live up to their promises and then there are people who don't. I can never guarantee that any company will be amazing, and I think you can only recommend people from your own experience. I think it is important to work with a company that listens to what you want, and even if it's hard to achieve your vision, they will just go for it. It might be a long process, cost a bit more, or cause loads of aggro, but you can still do it.

How to

CREATE A MOOD BOARD

Sometimes I will create a mood board for a room that I'm decorating, especially if it's a big project. You can remind yourself of why you are changing the room, where your inspiration has come from, and how you would like it to look.

I gather images from Pinterest and Instagram, collect scraps of fabric, take pictures on my phone when I am out and about, and if I like something that I see, I will always ask what it is and where it is from, then make a note on my phone. Then I put it all in one place in a notebook or drawing pad. For big projects, I'll create a pinboard and put it in the room that I'm decorating, so the vision of what I am trying to achieve doesn't get lost along the way. It helps you to keep going, because when you look at the mood board you remember that eventually it will all be worth it!

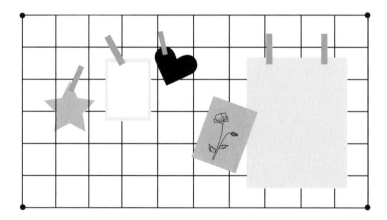

ALWAYS HAGGLE

Unless the project is something very specialist or I am buying from a small business, I will always haggle. I think a lot of the time we accept a price, but I don't think a 'final price' is ever a final price. There is always negotiation to be had.

If it's a big business and there is competition, I will always ask for a better price. I'll just say, 'So if that's the price you are giving me, what is the best price I can get?' If you have a fixed budget, what extras can they add in for that price? Don't be afraid to ask how you can bring the cost down. I think with big purchases, you can often remove around 10 per cent of the full price.

I think most big companies would rather have a sale with less commission than no sale at all. Always get different quotes, and if you like one company more than the others but it has a higher quote, ask if they will match the lower quote.

KEEP IT

I always recycle whenever possible but if I have anything that might be of use in the future I will keep it. From bits of wood to old handles, if you have space, keep what you can as you never know when you might need it. But if you think you'll never use your old things, there are places you can give stuff away, like Freecycle, or sell on old bits and bobs, like eBay or Gumtree. Someone else's rubbish is always another one's treasure!

DESIGN A KITCHEN

If you are going to spend big money on a kitchen, I think you really should have exactly what you want. There are millions of things to consider when you are thinking about the room, especially the shape of the kitchen – whether it is L-shaped, U-shaped, G-shaped, a galley, single wall, if you have an island etc. Then there is the choice of fitted versus free-standing furniture, open shelves, integrated appliances, display cabinets and so on. There are loads and loads of different worktop materials and flooring options. It can be a bit overwhelming at first to say the least!

It is important to count your cupboards and work out what space you need – for pans, plates, glassware, cutlery, food etc. If you have the space, write down everything you want to keep in your kitchen and designate a space for it and where you want it to go. For example, you will probably want the cups near the kettle and the fridge not far from the oven. This can even work for smaller kitchens because it will help you work out what you really need to keep at hand in your kitchen and what you can let go of or store elsewhere.

Take your time, so you are not rushed into making any decisions. When I was designing our kitchen, I thought about how I wanted to be in it; for example, I wanted to be able to look out of the window into the garden whilst standing at the sink. Some of the jobs in the kitchen are mundane, repetitive, and boring. So, if you can, make them a bit more enjoyable – if I can wash up and look at the kids playing outside – it doesn't feel as crappy a job. In your existing kitchen, really think about how you use it and what really bothers you about it, or how you could position things in a better way to work for you.

Builders and kitchen suppliers will tell you what you can and can't have but, in my experience, they won't tell you the more difficult stuff that they can do but you have to ask for! For example, in my utility room, I had to ask for the units to go right up to the ceiling. With most 'standard' kitchens, the units will sit underneath the ceiling and there will be a space there. I've found that we just shove stuff on top of the cupboards and it looks really ugly.

It is much harder to achieve things like this, especially in an older house like ours where the ceilings might not be completely level or there are curves, and the gaps are harder to fill. But, often, it can be done if you ask. For example, I think plinths (the boards at the bottom of cabinets in fitted kitchens) are wasted space, so in both our utility room and the kitchen, I asked for plinth drawers. Instead of having plinth boards, ask them to put those plinths on runners – and it's a drawer. Automatically you have a whole level of usable space underneath your kitchen that you didn't have before. It is possible in 99 per cent of kitchens. The kitchen company might say, 'I don't know, I don't know,' but push for it and say you don't want the kitchen unless they do that.

WHAT COMPANY SHOULD YOU USE?

When it came to deciding on what company to use for our utility room and kitchen, it was hard. We have used trade kitchen companies before, and they are great if you want a cheaper kitchen and are working with a builder. Your builder will be able to get trade prices, but these companies only have a standard set of kitchens, so there is less opportunity to design the space exactly how you want it. Then there are the super-expensive and uber-posh kitchens: nice as they are, and as much as I would love that, it is not practical for our family with young kids, and they are very, very expensive.

The company that we went with were Wren Kitchens. In terms of price, they were somewhere in the middle, but they had just what I wanted for our house. I wanted to keep the country style in our kitchen, with oak units and white units, and some detail on the oak.

They had all of that. Also, because they started on the utility room first, I got an impression of how they worked. They kept to their deadlines, were punctual, and were really nice to work with.

WHERE TO START?

Before I designed anything, I went in to see if they had the wood, units, worktops, certain pull-out cupboards, and handles and accessories that I like. It is important to make sure that they have the unit colour or type of wood you want. I wanted to mix and match with my colours, with white and oak, so it is two-tone and it is not very easy to find a high-street kitchen with light oak units. I think from being crazy about having things organised I knew what I needed and what I wanted to achieve with my kitchen to make my life easier. I needed to know I had full control over it. Sometimes you buy a full kitchen and you don't actually get to pick and choose the smaller details of the kitchen, so for me, it was important to choose a company that allowed me to have my say over the finer points.

When it comes to worktops, again, think about the materials, colours, or grain that you like. For cleaning, granite or stone is always my top choice. I find wood harder to clean and it never really feels fresh. Our old kitchen worktop at Pickle Cottage was a composite-type material and was good, but I found that it stained very easily; for example, when we had a curry and I splashed korma on there, I had to use acetone or some other ridiculous cleaning material to get it out. That kind of stuff is really important.

The flooring is also another decision – again, there are loads of options from slate, granite, porcelain and ceramic tiles, to wood flooring (this includes both engineered wood and solid wood), or laminate flooring. I wanted a tile with texture and grooves but I also wanted something that was easy to maintain with four kids and the dogs. I found the perfect porcelain tiles – Lappato 800x800mm – that looked matt with different tones that are still smooth and easy to keep clean. I chose a warm and inviting sandy stone colour and I am so happy with them.

A kitchen is a huge investment, so you have to just love it. Make sure you love every part of it.

PLANNING YOUR KITCHEN LAYOUT

In terms of the layout, we moved the sink under the window looking out onto the garden, with the best views. Nothing like a bit of washing up from a sink with a view. Our kitchen already had two very long windows, so we wanted to replicate that but also have corner bifold doors, so we can open the whole corner. Glazing is an important part of any renovation and getting it right will bring you such a lot of satisfaction.

We also had enough space for two dishwashers. I know this is a complete and utter luxury but we are a big family, and if I was going to have space for anything extra, it needed to be another dishwasher. With two, I can put all our dishes on in one go without also having to wash up anything that wouldn't fit into just one.

DO YOU NEED PLANNING PERMISSION?

You will need to think about this. We didn't need planning permission because there was already a roof and it was just an open bit of the house. We just took out the corner of the kitchen and built into the open space that had previously been a kind of porch area.

An architect will tell you what you can and can't do, and whether you need to apply for planning permission. Your architect will be able to tell you the likelihood of it going through or if you are going to struggle. If they say you are likely to get permission, I would say to provisionally book your builder because the good ones are often very busy. If the architect says the planning application process is going to take six to eight weeks, make sure you book your builder for eight weeks' time. Then you're good to go.

MANAGE A BUILD

If you have enough money to hire a project manager to get it all off your plate, then go for it. It's not something I would pay for, though, as I would rather do it myself and invest that money elsewhere. If you do manage a project yourself then you need to be really engaged in making sure your builder does exactly what you want and hits their deadlines.

You will want to get in an electrician, plumber, and windows person to do those things that you simply cannot do yourself. Sometimes your builder will coordinate all these other trades, so try to develop a really good relationship with your builder.

If you are out at work when they are in your house, agree on a time for them to FaceTime you each day to tell you what they are doing and where in the schedule they are. Get them to send you regular pictures and messages so you are always in the loop. Tell them, 'If you are ever thinking about doing X, Y or Z, then ring or text me.' Try to find a builder who will communicate with you constantly. And be crystal clear in all your communications with them.

I think it's great to be around if you possibly can. I even made my amazingly patient builder let me have a go at plastering! I only managed to do one wall in about three hours. There was a big window in it so it was basically a big picture frame's worth! I'd have loved to do the whole thing myself but I think my new kitchen would probably then have lots of wonky walls.

Little things I love ♡

PAINT SPRAYER

Paint sprayers are amazing for painting large areas.
I have bought a Wagner Airless ControlPro 350 M Paint
Sprayer and called it Steve after my builder! I would
recommend renting one first and seeing how you go.
Investment-wise, it only makes sense to buy one if you
have loads of painting to do. The one I bought was
expensive. There are cheaper (and more expensive)
models out there but I saw mine as an investment
because we have so many larger spaces to spray.

Using a paint sprayer is much quicker and I prefer
the overall finish. I used Tikkurila UK paint with it and it
sprays through the gun and washes out so easily.
It takes time to get the hang of it and it is really
important to do the right preparation because you will
need very carefully to tape up the bits that you do not
want to be sprayed. Overall though, I love it.

ALWAYS FIGHT FOR WHAT YOU WANT...

I know I've said it before but I really believe that you should have exactly what you want in your house, especially in a room like the kitchen where you spend loads of time.

I made sure our kitchen was exactly what I wanted right down to the smallest details, like having brass fittings, rather than silver. I started with silver but as the kitchen started to be fitted, I decided that brass was just a bit warmer and looked better. We used a lovely small business called Rural Ranges to switch the silver fittings on the Aga to brass ones. It was a much more complex job than I had imagined and they were brilliant and took care of every little detail. Audrey will always be at the heart of the kitchen, so I wanted her look to tie in with everything else and fit perfectly. I also plan to spray the silver fittings of the lights gold.

Always remember that you don't have to buy everything from the kitchen company you are using. You can shop around and get something from other places if that's what you prefer. I bought our sink, which sits within the main island, separately because it has an integrated chopping board, colander and waste disposal unit.

You can create a bespoke look for your kitchen for so much less than buying from an expensive kitchen brand. I asked a small business that I buy things from to create a cutlery tray for one of my drawers for a fraction of the price it would cost from a luxury designer. It is those small touches that turn an average-price kitchen into a very expensive one but if you are a bit clever about it, you can create these details like interesting cupboards or cupboard inserts more easily. You don't have to spend a small fortune to get the same look.

DECIDE WHAT GOES WHERE

My top tip would be to live in your kitchen for a while before deciding where to place things. You need to work out what you go to most frequently, and from where.

So, for example, my tea and coffee-making space is the cupboard opposite the sink where there is a hot tap. Everything I need to make hot drinks is in there, including a coffee machine. I had a real think about what would make my life easier, so I added a little bin for tea bags because there is nothing more annoying that dripping tea all over the floor on the way to the bin! I have also put some cereal in there because it is an easy-access cupboard for the kids. Think about the things that are likely to annoy you and try to find solutions.

There are other things you might like to think about to make your kitchen 'flow' and work for you: knives, chopping boards, and a food compost caddy (if you need one) should be near the food prep areas and your cutlery and crockery should be in the main part of your kitchen within easy reach – and near the dishwasher! The pots, pans and appliances that you use a lot should be stored in the main part of your kitchen – I am putting mine in my deep drawers. I am also going to experiment with hanging some pans up and see how it looks. I am lucky enough to have space in our utility room, so anything I do not use every day, like some baking items, can go in there.

You don't need a new kitchen to give you the excuse to re-organise. I think that is so satisfying once in a while to clear everything out, clean your cupboards, and re-organise to make your life easier!

Little things I love ♡

AUDREY THE AGA

When we moved into Pickle Cottage there was already
an AGA in the kitchen, which we loved as it warmed the
whole house. But it was old and used a huge amount of
gas so when we ripped out the kitchen, we sent it off to be
repurposed. We then switched to Audrey – a new electric
AGA – to save energy! And I am totally in love with her.

My top tip would be do not be afraid to just have a go with
your AGA. Say you have a cupcake recipe and it tells you to,
'Preheat your oven to 200°C,' you can't set a temperature on
an Aga. It is what it is. I would say to put your cupcakes in
and just keep having a look. You have to trust it will go OK.
There are some great AGA cookbooks out there. Mary Berry
has one that I have enjoyed reading and I also bought a
beginner's guide from AGA itself, which has been fab.

An AGA is for cooking but I've found it incredibly useful
for other reasons. Rex is always splashing in puddles, so
I hook his little trainers onto the AGA to dry them out.
My kids loved the old one. The boys always put their
school jumpers on it to warm them up before school.

ORGANISE THE
UNDER SINK CUPBOARD

The excitement I felt getting my tap to tidy on and organising all the cleaning products that I now store under my new kitchen sink was almost too much!

First, I put some magnetic sticky strips in the cupboard underneath to hang up my cloths using little pegs – and the adventure started! I think hanging up your cloths is a great idea because it make sort of curtain that hides all the ugly pipework.

Next, I decanted all my products into clear boxes, jars and bottles and labelled each one so that I can see at a glance exactly what I have or need to restock. This cupboard includes stuff I use all the time like dishwasher tablets and salt, surface spray, washing up liquid, white vinegar for cleaning, cloths and scourers. It can be tempting to shove too much stuff under the sink and end up not knowing what you have. Make it pretty, keep it tidy and don't clog up the space!

I always try to use eco-friendly products that do not contain harsh chemicals (particularly sprays), so I know I am trying in my own small way to help the environment. I also try to buy in bulk where possible, which means less packaging (see page 197). I then refill my containers as and when I need to, so there is less waste.

If you have small children, I would 100 per cent recommend putting child safety locks on the cupboard under the sink. Even eco-friendly cleaning products contain some chemicals, so you want to make sure small children can't accidentally get into here.

... AND GIVE IT TIME!

When planning your kitchen, you don't have to decide on your
fixtures and fittings straight away. Be prepared to give it some
time. It can be really hard to know exactly what you want until
the kitchen shell is in. I think you should wait until your kitchen
is being fitted and ask to see the different fixtures against it and
then make those important decisions after that. You can feel
pressured into making a 'final' decision really early on and having
a complete plan but you might change your mind or see the
kitchen slightly differently once it is there. So, in my experience,
just give yourself the time you need and don't be rushed into
making a plan too soon.

Your Project

Create your Own Moodboard ♡

KITCHEN

Create your Own Moodboard ♡

— LIVING ROOM

Create your Own Moodboard ♡

— BATHROOM

Create your Own Moodboard ♡

— BEDROOM

Things I ♡ Need to Buy

☐ ....

☐ ....

☐ ....

☐ ....

☐ ....

☐ ....

☐ ....

☐ ....

☐ ....

Things I ♡ Need to Buy

- [ ] ....
- [ ] ....
- [ ] ....
- [ ] ....
- [ ] ....
- [ ] ....
- [ ] ....
- [ ] ....
- [ ] ....

- [ ] ....
- [ ] ....
- [ ] ....
- [ ] ....
- [ ] ....
- [ ] ....
- [ ] ....
- [ ] ....
- [ ] ....

Things I ♡ Need to Buy

☐ ....   ☐ ....

☐ ....   ☐ ....

☐ ....   ☐ ....

☐ ....   ☐ ....

☐ ....   ☐ ....

☐ ....   ☐ ....

☐ ....   ☐ ....

☐ ....   ☐ ....

☐ ....   ☐ ....

Things I ♡
Need to Buy

- [ ] ....
- [ ] ....
- [ ] ....
- [ ] ....
- [ ] ....
- [ ] ....
- [ ] ....
- [ ] ....
- [ ] ....

MY ROOM
Checklist

ROOM: ....

☐ Getting started

☐ On my way

☐ Almost done

☐ Finished!

ROOM: ....

☐ Getting started

☐ On my way

☐ Almost done

☐ Finished!

MY ROOM
Checklist

ROOM: ....

☐ Getting started

☐ On my way

☐ Almost done

☐ Finished!

ROOM: ....

☐ Getting started

☐ On my way

☐ Almost done

☐ Finished!

MY ROOM
Checklist

ROOM: ....

☐ Getting started
☐ On my way
☐ Almost done
☐ Finished!

ROOM: ....

☐ Getting started
☐ On my way
☐ Almost done
☐ Finished!

MY ROOM
Checklist

ROOM: ....

☐ Getting started

☐ On my way

☐ Almost done

☐ Finished!

ROOM: ....

☐ Getting started

☐ On my way

☐ Almost done

☐ Finished!

Notes ♡

Notes ♡

PICKLE COTTAGE Q&A

Q: How do you cope with the mess?

A: I think you just have to be prepared for it. Don't underestimate how hard building work is going to be, and how hard it is going to be to live in the house while it's going on. Prepare yourself for the worst and then you won't be overwhelmed when you realise it is a lot to deal with. Also, don't kill yourself trying to clean the house all the time. Let it get dusty because the dust will only settle the next day and you will have to do it again. Wait until certain big projects are completed and then give the house a really thorough deep clean.

Q: How do you balance the work or kids and DIY?

A: It is important to get to the stage when you accept that things might not get done quickly because DIY is not your full-time job; you can't dedicate every moment of the day to it. You must celebrate the small victories. Be proud of yourself even if you haven't necessarily completed as much as you wanted or hoped for. Big yourself up and tell yourself you have done a great job, because it is not easy, and you are not going to get it all done at once. Look at what you have actually done – however small or unfinished. I take a lot of photos when I am doing anything in the house. Looking back at 'before' photos, I can instantly see just how far things have progressed and this gives me the energy to keep going.

Q: How can I make my home feel special if I am renting?

A: There are loads of ways to make your home feel really special when you are renting. I have mentioned a few ideas throughout the book. The boys' kitchen is a good example of what I would do to a kitchen of a rental property – painting the units, changing the handles and sticking a vinyl covering over the worksurfaces gives an almost instant revamp (see page 94). In a tired bathroom, using specialist tile paint is a quick and cheap way to freshen things up (see page 126), as is renewing the grouting (see page 122). For walls, you can buy peel-on-peel-off wallpaper that you don't have to stick on with paste, which can totally transform a room. We used that in a house in **Sort Your Life Out**. You don't have to drill holes in walls to hang your favourites prints or photos: you can use Command Strips or hooks that stick to the wall (see page 124). But if you do want to put up any floating shelves or hang a mirror, it's a great idea to learn how to 'make good' by filling a hole in a wall (see page 217). It is not as hard as it sounds. Then you know you are capable of using nails and screws and then you can fill any holes afterwards. As you know, I am big on accessories. I love my fejkas and swinger's grass. Go all out with your favourite accessories to make your space really personal, no matter how long you might be there for. You can always take these things on to your next property. The same goes for floor rugs, which are the perfect way to cover up an ugly carpet and give some extra cosiness to a space. I would say to always speak to your landlord, because why would they be upset that you are taking the trouble to decorate? It's good for them too. Just run it by them first and talk to them about your plans.

Q: What if other people don't like what I've done to my home?

A: Well, all I would say to that is: it's a good job they don't have to live there! People have a lot to say about what I have done and am doing in Pickle Cottage. Most of the time it's nice but there is always the odd one. (Hi Wilma!) I think it says more about them than it does about me. If bitching about my house makes them happy, they can crack on! No-one should make you feel a certain way about something, so if you love it, sod 'em! Sometimes others are right when pointing out where I have gone wrong. In that case, I just start again!

Q: How often do you re-paint?

A: I only re-paint once every few years. You learn what are the busy areas that attract fingerprints and the places where you might need a more durable or washable emulsion as you go along. If you do a good job, your paintwork will stay fresh for at least a couple of years.

Final ♡ Thought

I hope you have enjoyed coming along on the journey of bringing Pickle Cottage back to life. The reason I decided to put pen to paper was that I never thought I would have the opportunity to own a house like this and turn it into a home.

It has been a once-in-a-lifetime experience and I have enjoyed every single second of pouring hard work, effort, sweat and – importantly – love into making this home truly ours.

More than anything I hope that this book makes you feel empowered and encouraged to go for it if you want to change something in your own home. Never be afraid. The ball is in your court! It is limitless and you don't have to spend loads of money. Your home is an expression of you – your interests, dreams, and the things you love. Even the smallest and simplest changes make your home unique and perfect – just like you!

Since some of my first changes to Pickle Cottage, I have gone on to make even more changes to some rooms. After loving my black and white bathroom for around a year, I created my dream mermaid bathroom with gold accents, shimmering tiles, and shell-shaped sinks. We had to save for it but I have always dreamed of having a walk-in shower and my dream has finally come true! It actually made me just as happy to create both bathrooms, so if you want to spruce something up and you have no budget, trust me, a bit of filler and a lick of paint can have the same effect and be just as exciting.

The pool is finally coming together after what has felt like forever and is now tiled with shiny mosaic-style tiles that glint in the sunlight. I created Rex his own dream dinosaur-themed bathroom and Joe his games room for his 40th birthday. Seeing their faces light up was honestly the best feeling ever. To see my dream home become a reality and have my family around me is truly magical.

Creating our dream forever home feels like the best experience. I'm so glad to have you alongside me for the ride, as your support means so, so much to me. Don't let your dreams just be dreams; I promise that you can achieve anything you want.

Love you to the moon and back,

Stace xxx

Index

Suppliers

RESEARCH & TUTORIALS

Google
Instagram
Pinterest
The Folding Lady on Instagram
YouTube

GENERAL DIY

B&Q – stores nationwide
www.diy.com

COMMAND STRIPS
Command.3m.co.uk

FROGTAPE
www.frogtape.co.uk

HOMEBASE – stores nationwide
www.homebase.co.uk

ROBERT DYAS – stores nationwide
www.robertdyas.co.uk

SCREWFIX – stores nationwide
www.screwfix.com

THE RANGE – stores nationwide
www.therange.co.uk

TOOLSTATION – stores nationwide
www.toolstation.com

UNIBOND – products stocked
in all major DIY stores, including
NoMoreNails adhesive and Re-New
grout sealant
www.unibond.co.uk

WICKES – stores nationwide
www.wickes.co.uk

TOOL HIRE

HSS HIRE – stores nationwide
www.hss.com

PAINT

DECO COLOR EPOXY KERAMIK –
epoxy waterproof spray paint
www.deco-color.com/products_en/
epoxy

DULUX
www.dulux.co.uk

FARROW & BALL
www.farrow-ball.com

FRENCHIC – al Fresco, mineral and
chalk paint
www.frenchicpaint.co.uk

SECURIT CHALKBOARD PAINT
www.securit.nl

TIKKURILA UK
www.tikkurila.co.uk

FURNITURE, HOMEWARES & ACCESSORIES

AMAZON
www.amazon.co.uk

THE BESPOKE CARPENTRY CO.
www.handmade-furniture.co.uk

BYBONHOMIE – fake flowers
www.bybonhomie.co.uk

DUNELM – stores nationwide
www.dunelm.com

EBAY
www.ebay.co.uk

FALL WITH GRACE
www.fallwithgrace.co.uk

FAMILY RULE
www.familyrule.co.uk

FENWICK
www.fenwick.co.uk

GARDEN TRADING COMPANY
www.gardentrading.co.uk

HOMESENSE – stores nationwide
www.homesense.com

HOMEZONE
www.homezone1.co.uk

IKEA – stores nationwide
www.ikea.com

JOSEPH JOSEPH
www.josephjoseph.com

MUTHA MAKER
www.muthamaker.com

NEXT HOME – stores nationwide
www.next.co.uk

PRETTY LITTLE HOME
www.prettylittlehome.co.uk

PRIMARK – stores nationwide
www.primark.com

SWANS AND BLUEBELLS – baby goods
www.swansandbluebells.com

THE CHESHIRE GIFT COMPANY
www.cheshiregiftcompany.co.uk

THE LABEL LADY
www.thelabellady.shop

THE LITTLE HOUSE OF RAINBOWS – baby goods
www.thelittlehouseofrainbows.co.uk

LIGHTING

LIGHTS4FUN
www.lights4fun.co.uk

PAGAZZI LIGHTING
www.pagazzi.com

FIREPLACE

FIREPLACE FACTORY
www.fireplace-factory.co.uk

KITCHEN

AGA
www.agaliving.com

RURAL RANGES
www.rural ranges.com

WREN KITCHENS
www.wrenkitchens.com

FITTED FURNITURE

LEWIS JAMES
www.lewis-james.co.uk
@lewisjamesbk

SHARPS – stores nationwide
www.sharps.co.uk

BATHROOM

THE CAST IRON BATH COMPANY
www.castironbath.co.uk

FLOORING

ABBOTT FLOORING
www.abbottflooringuk.co.uk

A CLARKE CARPETS AND FLOORING
www.aclarkecarpets.co.uk

FREELANDS TILES
www.freelands-tiles.co.uk

WOODPECKER
www.woodpeckerflooring.co.uk

WINDOWS

BDC ALUMINIUM
www.bcdaluminium.co.uk

SWIMMING POOLS

BESPOKE SWIMMING POOLS
www.bespokeswimmingpools.com
@bespoke_swimming_pools

ECO-CLEANING

BIO-D
www.biod.co.uk
ECOVER
www.ecover.com

METHOD
www.methodproducts.co.uk

SELLING & REPURPOSING SITES

FREECYCLE
www.freecycle.org

EBAY
www.ebay.co.uk

GUMTREE
www.gumtree.com

TRADESPEOPLE

Checkatrade.com
Ratedpeople.com
Trustatrader.com

BUILDERS

SJS LIMITED
www.sjsweb.co.uk
@sjsltd

STEVE HOPE SERVICES
www.stevehopeservices.co.uk
@stevehope.decorating

SW NICHOLLS
www.swnicholls.co.uk
@sw.nicholls

ELECTRICIAN

HIGGINS ELECTRICAL SERVICES
www.higginselectricalservicesltd.co.uk
@higgins_electrical_services

Thank Yous

Thank you to my amazing publishing team at Ebury: Lizzy, Laura, Lisa, Steph, Abby, Alice, Claire, Lucy, Hannah and Aslan. This book is so close to my heart, and you've taken such good care of it.

Thank you to Emily, Molly and Amanda at YMU Group.

Georgina Rodgers, thank you for watching me build and drill and paint Pickle Cottage, and help me write this book. There was so much information I wanted to share, and you've helped me get everything down on the page.

Thank you to the incredibly talented designers – Nikki and Emma at Nic&Lou – and the illustrators – Natalia and Katharine – who've made Pickle Cottage come alive in this book.

As always, the Famo is everything: Mum, Dad, Karen, Jemma, Matthew, Joshy, SamSam, Ray, Aaron, Kiffy Sharna, Casie and Dan ... to the moon and back everyone. Pickle Cottage wouldn't be what it is today without you ... and the love and laughs.

Joe, what a year we've had. Thank you for being my person, for now and for always. I am truly blessed to share my life with you.

Zachary, Leighton, Harry, Rex and Rose: our beautiful children. Every day, I love you more and more ... I didn't think that was possible! To the moon and back, my everythings.

I can't forget Peanut and Teddy, you bring such joy and complete our Pickle Cottage family. And thank you to Theo, who I miss every day.

Also by Stacey Solomon

STACEY SOLOMON

Tap to tidy

ORGANISING, CRAFTING
& CREATING HAPPINESS
IN A MESSY WORLD

Ebury Press, an imprint of Ebury Publishing,
20 Vauxhall Bridge Road,
London SW1V 2SA

Ebury Press is part of the Penguin Random House group of companies whose
addresses can be found at global.penguinrandomhouse.com

Illustrations on pages 2, 4–5, 13, 24–5, 29, 31, 44, 48–9, 53, 69, 76–7, 81, 91, 93, 96–7,
103, 118–19, 132, 138–9, 145, 151, 157, 161, 166–7, 188–9, 193, 195, 212–13, 221, 225, 229,
232–3, 247 © Natalia Sanabria and Katharine Asher
Illustrations on pages 34, 41, 42, 43, 56–7, 61, 64, 85, 90, 95, 101, 107, 109, 115, 123, 125,
127, 129, 143, 147, 149, 154, 172–3, 175, 177, 181, 184, 209, 211, 217 © Kuo Kang Chen
All other illustrations Shutterstock

First published by Ebury Press in 2022
www.penguin.co.uk

A CIP catalogue record for this book is available from the British Library

ISBN: 9781529148664

Designed by Studio Nic&Lou

Colour origination by Altaimage, London
Printed and bound in Italy by Graphicom, S.r.l.

The authorised representative in the EEA is Penguin Random House Ireland,
Morrison Chambers, 32 Nassau Street, Dublin D02 YH68

Penguin Random House is committed to a sustainable future for our business, our readers
and our planet. This book is made from Forest Stewardship Council® certified paper.